ARAB AMERICAN VOICES

ARAB AMERICAN VOICES

Loretta Hall

AN IMPRINT OF THE GALE GROUP

DETROIT · SAN FRANCISCO · LONDON
BOSTON · WOODBRIDGE, CT

Arab American Voices

Loretta Hall

Staff

Sonia Benson, *U·X·L Senior Editor*
Elizabeth Des Chenes and Carol DeKane Nagel, *U·X·L Contributing Editors*
Thomas L. Romig, *U·X·L Publisher*

Shalice Shah-Caldwell, *Permissions Associate (Text and pictures)*
Rita Wimberley, *Senior Buyer*
Evi Seoud, *Assistant Production Manager*
Dorothy Maki, *Manufacturing Manager*

Michelle DiMercurio, *Senior Art Director*
Cynthia Baldwin, *Product Design Manager*

The Graphix Group, *Typesetting*

Library of Congress Cataloging-in-Publication Data

Arab American voices / Loretta Hall.
    p. cm.
Includes bibliographical references and index.

  Summary: Twenty primary source documents from speeches, memoirs, poems, novels, and autobiographies present the words of Americans with roots in Lebanon, Syria, Palestine, Iraq, Egypt, and other Arab nations.

ISBN 0-7876-2956-1

  I. Arab Americans—History Sources Juvenile literature. 2. Arab Americans Biography Juvenile literature. 3. Speeches, addresses, etc., American—Arab American authors Juvenile literature. [1. Arab Americans—History Sources. 2. Arab American Biography.]

I. Title.

E184. A65H36 1999
973'.04927—cd21

                              99-37500
                              CIP

Printed in the United States of America

10 9 8 7 6 5 4 3 2 1

Contents

Reader's Guide

Through twenty-seven full or excerpted speeches, newspaper accounts, poems, memoirs, interviews, and other materials by and about Arab Americans, *Arab American Voices* explores issues central to what it means to be of Arab descent in the United States today. The primary sources featured range from Kahlil Gibran's poem "Dead Are My People," which recalls the brutal conditions under which Arabs lived under Ottoman rule prior to World War I, to James Abourezk's speech outlining the impact of the Arab–Israeli conflict on the collective psyche of Arab Americans. Also included is Ghassan Saleh and Tom Quigley's call for tolerance toward Arabs and Arab Americans in the aftermath of the Oklahoma City bombing as well as an interview with Arab American girls struggling to maintain their Arab traditions while attending an American high school.

Arab American Voices is broken into seven sections, including "The First Wave of Arab Immigrants," "Arab Americans, Civil Rights, and Prejudice," and "Religion in Arab American Communities." Each of the twenty–five entries is accompanied by an introduction and biographical and historical information, a document–specific glossary, and sources for further reading. The volume is illustrated with thirty-four black-and-white photographs and features a timeline of important events in Arab American history and a subject index.

Related reference sources:

Arab American Biography profiles seventy-five Arab Americans notable for their achievements in a variety of fields, ranging from social activism to sports, academia to politics, entertainment to science, and religion to the military. Early immigrants as well as contemporary figures are among those included. Black-and-white photographs accompany most entries.

Arab American Encyclopedia explores the history and culture of the diverse groups of Americans who trace their ancestry to one or more of the twenty-one Arab countries. The *Encyclopedia* is organized into nineteen subject chapters, including immigration, religion, employment, education, family, health, civil rights, music, and literature, and contains more than seventy black-and-white photographs.

Comments and Suggestions

We welcome your comments on this work as well as your suggestions for topics to be featured in future editions of *Arab American Voices*. Please write: Editors, *Arab American Voices*, U•X•L, 27500 Drake Rd., Farmington Hills, MI 48331–3535; call toll-free: 1–800–877–4253; fax: 248–414–5043; or send e-mail via www.galegroup.com.

Timeline

1878   The first wave of Arab American immigration to the United States begins; it consists almost entirely of Syrians and Lebanese.

1914   **Abraham Mitrie Rihbany** writes *A Far Journey* about his transition from a Syrian Orthodox boy to an American Protestant minister.

1916   **Kahlil Gibran** writes "Dead Are My People" to encourage Arab immigrants to help the starving people in Syria.

1921   The United States Government enacts its first law limiting the number of immigrants by their country of origin.

1877
Thomas Edison patents
the phonograph

1898
Spanish-American
War begins

1920
Women are
granted the
right to vote

1875   1900   1925

1924 The Immigration Act of 1924 limits Syrian immigration to 100 persons per year.

1932 The Eastern Federation of Clubs unites Arab organizations in many communities, emphasizing their common ethnicity.

1936 **Hannah Sabbagh Shakir** participates in a labor union strike seeking better treatment of employees at textile mills where many Syrian immigrants work.

1939 **Salom Rizk** begins a national speaking tour to inspire teenagers to be proud of being Americans.

1948 The second wave of Arab immigration to the United States begins as Israel is founded on Palestinian lands and hundreds of thousands of Palestinian Arabs are forced out of their homes.

1956 **Michael A. Shadid** writes *Crusading Doctor.*

1965 The United States stops limiting immigrants on the basis of their country of origin, leading to the beginning of the third wave of Arab immigration.

1967 Israel captures more Arab land in the Six Day War, forcing many more Palestinians away from their homes.

1970 Lebanese American poet **H. S. "Sam" Hamod** writes "After the Funeral of Assam Hamady" about his experience as a Muslim Arab in America.

1970 The American Druze Society forms the Committee on Religious Affairs to publish books about Druze history and faith.

1973 The Organization of Petroleum Exporting Countries (OPEC), comprised largely of Arab members, refuses to sell oil to the United States, creating an energy cri-

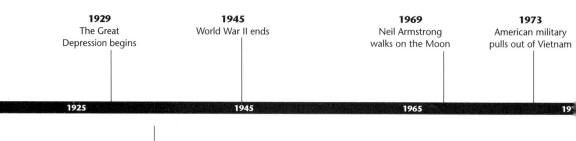

1929	1945	1969	1973
The Great Depression begins	World War II ends	Neil Armstrong walks on the Moon	American military pulls out of Vietnam

1925   1945   1965   19'

sis. **Mojahid Daoud** returns to America after a one-year sojourn in his native Jordan to find widespread resentment toward Arabs.

1975   A sixteen-year-long civil war begins in Lebanon; news reports during this period lead Americans to think of Lebanese people only in terms of violence and destruction.

1978   The Foreign Intelligence Surveillance Act (FISA) of 1978 becomes law.

1978   Syrian American Lisa Halaby marries the king of Jordan and becomes an international spokeswoman for modern Arab women.

1980   Former senator **James Abourezk** establishes the American-Arab Anti-Discrimination Committee to unite Arab Americans and raise their self-image.

1980   American Muslims begin a campaign to build private schools where their children can learn Islamic values and the Arabic language.

1982   To a group of Arab Americans **Gladys Shibley Sadd** relates childhood memories of growing up in the Arab community of Boston at the turn of the twentieth century.

1982   Operations begin at Jordan's huge, new potash refinery, which was designed and built by a company owned by Lebanese American **Joseph J. Jacobs.**

1985   Lebanese terrorists hijack a TWA airplane carrying 153 people, killing one American passenger. This and several later hijackings make Americans feel fear and resentment toward people of Arab ancestry.

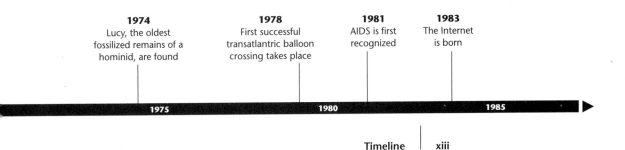

1974	1978	1981	1983
Lucy, the oldest fossilized remains of a hominid, are found	First successful transatlantric balloon crossing takes place	AIDS is first recognized	The Internet is born

1975   1980   1985

1987 Palestinian Arab **Anton Shammas** leaves Israel to come to America, seeking safety from Jewish extremists for himself and his family.

c. 1990 Linda Walbridge interviews a number of Arab immigrants living in Michigan including **Anisa**, who had emigrated with her husband from Yemen in the 1970s.

1990 **Nezar Andary** is asked to represent the American Druze Youth at the American Druze Society's national convention. He delivers a speech on issues concerning Druze youth in America.

1991 After Iraq invades Kuwait, the United Nations, led by the United States, launches the Gulf War to drive the invaders out. **Shameen Rassam Amal** is afraid to return to her native Iraq from a visit to the United States.

1992 Immigration to the United States from Iraq triples after the United Nations forbids that country to sell the oil it produces; many people flee Iraq because of shortages of food and medical supplies.

1992 **Naomi Shihab Nye** writes "Banned Poem" about Israel's treatment of Palestinian Arabs.

1993 The governments of Israel and the landless state of Palestine sign the Oslo Agreement outlining steps toward peace between their nations.

1994 Palestinian American **Lisa Suhair Majaj** writes "Boundaries: Arab/Americans" about her search for a personal identity.

1995 A spectacular bombing in Oklahoma City, Oklahoma, sparks fears of Arab terrorist attacks in the United States, even though Arabs were not involved in this explosion; **Ghassan Saleh** and Tom Quigley write a plea for tolerance toward Arab Americans.

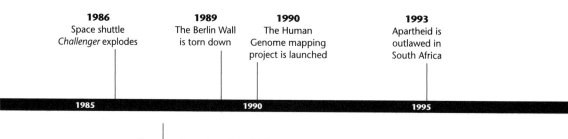

1986
Space shuttle
Challenger explodes

1989
The Berlin Wall
is torn down

1990
The Human
Genome mapping
project is launched

1993
Apartheid is
outlawed in
South Africa

1985   1990   1995

1996 The Antiterrorism and Effective Death Penalty Act (AEDPA) of 1996 becomes law. Two years later **Zana Macki** airs her views on its secret-evidence provisions, which are used most often against Arabs.

1996 After viewing *Executive Decision,* a film in which Arabs are stereotypically portrayed as terrorists, **Magdoline Asfahani** writes an essay for *Newsweek* calling attention to the true danger: discrimination against Arabs and other ethnic groups.

1996 Charlene Eisenlohr publishes her interview of **Adolescent Arab Girls in an American High School** in which the girls discuss the difficulties they face trying to adhere to the traditional customs of their parents' native lands in America.

1997 Evelyn Shakir interviews a number of Arab American women and collects their stories in *Bint Arab;* **Mona,** a young Palestinian Arab who finds honor in her political work, is among those whose stories Shakir tells.

1997 **Maha Ezzeddine** wins the American Muslim Council's essay contest with "What Ramadan Means to Me."

1998 **Atif Harden** urges Congress to try new strategies for stopping terrorism.

1998 **Jamil I. Toubbeh** writes *Day of the Long Night: A Palestinian Refugee Remembers the Nakba.*

1999 U.S. House of Representatives begins considering a bill that would repeal the secret evidence provisions of the AEDPA.

1999 Ehud Barak becomes prime minister of Israel, renewing hopes for peace between Israel and its Arab neighbors.

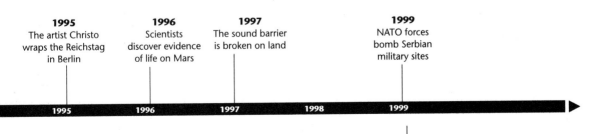

1995
The artist Christo wraps the Reichstag in Berlin

1996
Scientists discover evidence of life on Mars

1997
The sound barrier is broken on land

1999
NATO forces bomb Serbian military sites

1995 1996 1997 1998 1999

Acknowledgments

The editors wish to thank the copyright holders of the excerpted documents included in *Arab American Voices* and the permissions managers of many book and magazine publishing companies for assisting us in securing reproduction rights. Following is a list of the copyright holders who have granted us permission to reproduce material in this volume. Every effort has been made to trace copyright, but if omissions have been made, please let us know.

Kahlil Gibran. From *Secrets of the Heart.* Translated by Anthony Rizcallah Ferris. Signet Books, 1947. Renewed 1974 by Philosophical Library, Inc. Reproduced by permission.

Salom Rizk. From *Syrian Yankee.* Doubleday, 1943. Copyright, 1943, renewed 1970 by Salom Rizk. All rights reserved. Reproduced by permission.

Hannah Sabbagh Shakir. From *Bint Arab: Arab and Arab American Women in the United States.* By Evelyn Shakir. Praeger, 1997. Copyright © 1997 by Evelyn Shakir. All rights reserved. Reproduced by permission of Greenwood Publishing Group, Inc., Westport, CT.

Quigley. © 1995 The Dallas Morning News. Reproduced by permission of the authors.

Magdoline Asfahani. *Newsweek,* December 2, 1996, for "Time to Look and Listen: Thanksgiving Reminds Us That Our Differences Unite Us and Make Us Unique as a Nation." © 1996 Newsweek, Inc. All rights reserved. Reproduced by permission.

Zana Macki. *Detroit News,* October 14, 1998, for "Take a Lesson from History and End Arab-American Discrimination before It's Too Late." Copyright © 1998, The Detroit News, a Gannett newspaper. Reproduced by permission.

James Abourezk. Arab-American University Graduates. Reproduced by permission.

H. S. "Sam" Hamod. From *Grape Leaves: A Century of Arab American Poetry.* Edited by Gregory Orfalea and Sharif Elmusa. University of Utah Press, 1988. Reproduced by permission.

Adolescent Arab Girls in an American High School. Interview by Charlene Joyce Eisenlohr. From *Family and Gender Among American Muslims: Issues Facing Middle Eastern Immigrants and Their Descendants.* Edited by Barbara C. Aswad and Barbara Bilgé. Temple University Press, 1996. Copyright © 1996 by Temple University. All rights reserved. Reproduced by permission.

Mona. From *Bint Arab: Arab and Arab American Women in the United States.* By Evelyn Shakir. Praeger, 1997. Copyright © 1997 by Evelyn Shakir. All rights reserved. Reproduced by permission of Greenwood Publishing Group, Inc., Westport, CT.

Lisa Suhair Majaj. From *Food For Our Grandmothers: Writings by Arab-American and Arab-Canadian Feminists.* Edited by Joanna Kadi. South End Press, 1994. Copyright © 1994 by Joanna Kadi. Reproduced by permission.

Abraham Mitrie Rihbany. From *A Far Journey.* Houghton Mifflin, 1914. Reproduced by permission.

Maha Ezzedine. American Muslim Council. Reproduced by permission.

Nezar Andary. *Our Heritage,* Fall 1990. American Druze Society (ADS). Reproduced by permission.

The First Wave of Arab Immigrants: 1878–1924

Arabs are people whose ancestral language is Arabic. Today there are twenty-one Arab countries in northern Africa and southwestern Asia. The Ottoman Empire, founded by Turkish tribes in the late thirteenth century, expanded into a vast territory that included large areas of Europe and Asia. The Ottomans conquered the Asian portion of the Arab world in the sixteenth century and controlled it until the end of World War I (1914–18), when their empire was dissolved.

When Arabs started coming to America in the late 1800s, they were listed on immigration records by many different terms, including Arabs, Syrians, Turks, Ottomans, and even Greeks. At that time, Syria was a province of the Ottoman Empire. Its local government was entrusted to religious groups, such as Maronite Catholics (an Arab community of Christians that accepts the pope as church leader) and the Druze (followers of a form of Islam), that were dominant in each region of the province. Lebanon was a region of Syria. Thus, an immigrant from Lebanon might correctly be called either Lebanese or Syrian.

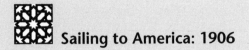

Sailing to America: 1906

During the first wave of Arab immigration, people traveled from Syria to America by ship. For most of them, the several-week voyage was extraordinarily difficult. George Hamid, who made the trip when he was ten years old, described it this way:

> Our quarters were cramped beyond imagination. The odor, heavy and ever-present, made us sick at first. Then we got used to it. . . .
>
> The food was the world's worst. The filth was knee-deep. No one attempted to clean up any of it during the time we were on the ship. There were no bed-clothes at all, but that was not so bad because we had no windows or ventilation and were roasting all the time. [My two cousins and I] roomed with one other person and a large variety of animal life. In two nights, Shaheen, who had the bottom bunk, had his fingernails and toenails chewed almost off by the rats. (George A. Hamid. *Circus.* New York: Sterling, 1950, p. 25.)

Between 1878 and 1924, a "first wave" of nearly 125,000 Arabs immigrated to the United States, almost exclusively from Syria (including Lebanon). Initially, most were men who came alone, intending to work in America for a few years and return to their families with the money they had saved. In fact, most of these men either stayed in America or returned later with their families. Eventually, entire families began migrating. After about 1900, as political tensions mounted in Europe and Asia prior to World War I, increasing numbers of Syrians came to the United States to escape hardships: the Turkish government was drafting the men into its army, those who spoke out against the government were sent to prison, the government took food and medical supplies from the people to support the army, and some natural crop failures made food even more scarce. Philosopher and poet **Kahlil Gibran**, who immigrated to the United States from Lebanon in 1902, became a spokesperson for the suffering people of Syria.

Salom Rizk, another Syrian immigrant of the World War I era, also became a public spokesperson. Although he powerfully described the plight of the Syrian people, his main message was directed at his fellow Americans. Having grown up in a different society, he noticed and appreciated things many people born in the United States take for granted.

Some first-wave Arab immigrants became public figures—writing, speaking, or building prominent businesses. Most, however, like **Hannah Sabbagh Shakir**, quietly spent their lives working and raising families. In recent years, first- and second-generation Syrian Americans (those whose parents or grandparents immigrated) have begun to explore their ethnic identity by searching out the stories of the early immigrants—stories mostly preserved in the memories of family members who listened as their elders told of their experiences. A few, like Shakir's daughter, published those stories so more people could share them.

Gladys Shibley Sadd and **Joseph J. Jacobs** are first-generation Arab Americans who shared their own memories with others outside their families through speeches and books. They described what it was like to grow up in the Syrian communities that developed in Boston, Massachusetts, and New York, New York, two of the main port cities where Arab immigrants landed in the United States.

After World War I ended, large numbers of immigrants poured into the United States from many countries devastated by the war. Jobs became harder to find as immigrants competed with Americans for work. In 1921 the U.S. government enacted a law limiting the number of people who could enter from each foreign country; the limit for Syrians was 925 per year. The Immigration Act of 1924 further reduced the number of immigrants who would be allowed to enter the United States: the limit for Syrians dropped to 100 per year, nearly ending Arab immigration until 1948, when a second wave of Arab immigrants began entering America.

Kahlil Gibran

"Dead Are My People"
Published in 1916

When Kahlil Gibran (1883–1931) came to the United States in 1894, Syrians saw America more as a land of opportunity than as a refuge from war or starvation. Even when Gibran returned to Lebanon four years later to attend college, he suffered from family tensions as least as much as he suffered from political pressures and economic problems. He came back to the United States in 1902, but he always considered himself a Syrian as well as an American.

During World War I (1914–18), the people in Lebanon suffered greatly as their food and medical supplies were taken for the use of soldiers of the Turkish Ottoman Empire, which controlled the region. Men were forced to join the Turkish army and fight in the war, and many of them were killed. People who spoke out against the government were sent to prison. At home in New York, Gibran was building a reputation as an artist and poet, but he was not yet earning enough to support himself, though a sponsor did give him money to live on so he could develop his talents. His life was far from luxurious, yet he realized how much worse conditions were in Lebanon.

"What can an exiled son do for his / Starving people, and of what value / Unto them is the lamentation of an / Absent poet?"

The ruins of a building in Damascus, Syria, after French forces bombed the civilian target, November 1925. Following World War I, French rule replaced Turkish rule in long-suffering Syria. *Reproduced by permission of Corbis/Bettmann–UPI.*

Beginning in 1914, Gibran sent money to Syria to help ease the suffering. By 1916, he was secretary of the Syrian–Mount Lebanon Relief Committee, actively seeking donations from other Syrian Americans. That is when he wrote "Dead Are My People," a poem that first appeared in an Arabic-language magazine published in New York.

In addition to collecting money for food and medical care, Gibran also encouraged Syrians and Lebanese to revolt against Turkey and fight for the right to govern themselves. He helped organize the Syrian–Mount Lebanon Volunteer Committee to encourage Arab Americans to join the French army, which was preparing to invade Syria. Even after World War I ended in 1918, Gibran continued to write poems and essays that would arouse the Syrians and Lebanese to demand self-rule. Beginning in the 1920s, he concentrated on writing spiritual books such as *The Prophet* and *Jesus, The Son of Man.*

Things to remember while reading "Dead Are My People":

- At least 100,000 people (one-fourth of the population) starved to death in Lebanon during World War I.

- In "Dead Are My People," Gibran expresses guilt about not staying in Lebanon with his suffering people, and he calls on his fellow immigrants to help those who are dying in the land they left.

"Dead Are My People"

(Written in exile during the famine in Syria)
"WORLD WAR I"

Gone are my people, but I exist yet,
Lamenting *them in my* ***solitude****. . . .*
Dead are my friends, and in their
Death my life is ***naught*** *but great*
Disaster.

The ***knolls*** *of my country are* ***submerged***
By tears and blood, for my people and
My beloved are gone, and I am here
Living as I did when my people and my
Beloved were enjoying life and the
Bounty *of life, and when the hills of*
My country were blessed and engulfed
By the light of the sun.

My people died from hunger, and he who
Did not perish from starvation was
Butchered with the sword; and I am
Here in this distant land, roaming
Amongst a joyful people who sleep
Upon soft beds, and smile at the days
While the days smile upon them. . . .

If I were hungry and living amid my
Famished *people, and persecuted among*
My ***oppressed*** *countrymen, the burden*

Lamenting: Mourning for.

Solitude: Aloneness.

Naught: Nothing.

Knolls: Small hills.

Submerged: Covered.

Bounty: Abundance, plenty.

Famished: Starving.

Oppressed: Downtrodden; spiritually broken.

Of the black days would be lighter
Upon my restless dreams, and the
Obscurity of the night would be less
Dark before my hollow eyes and my
Crying heart and my wounded soul.
For he who shares with his people
Their sorrow and agony will feel a
Supreme comfort created only by
Suffering in sacrifice. And he will
Be at peace with himself when he dies
Innocent with his fellow innocents.

But I am not living with my hungry
*And **persecuted** people who are walking*
In the procession of death toward
***Martyrdom**. . . . I am here beyond the*
Broad seas living in the shadow of
***Tranquility**, and in the sunshine of*
Peace. . . . I am afar from the pitiful
Arena and the distressed and cannot
*Be proud of **aught**, not even of my own*
Tears.

What can an exiled son do for his
Starving people, and of what value
*Unto them is the **lamentation** of an*
Absent poet?. . .

My people and your people, my Syrian
Brother, are dead. . . . What can be
Done for those who are dying? Our
Lamentations will not satisfy their
Hunger, and our tears will not quench
Their thirst; what can we do to save
Them from between the iron paws of
Hunger? My brother, the kindness
Which compels you to give a part of
Your life to any human who is in the
Shadow of losing his life is the only
***Virtue** which makes you worthy of the*
Light of day and the peace of the
Night. . . . Remember, my brother,
That the coin which you drop into
The withered hand stretching toward

Persecuted: Victimized.

Martyrdom: Dying for a righteous cause.

Tranquility: Peacefulness.

Aught: Anything.

Lamentation: Expression of grief.

Virtue: Act of goodness.

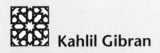

Kahlil Gibran

Kahlil Gibran (1883–1931) was twelve years old when his mother brought him, his brother, and his two sisters to America in search of a better life. His father was a lazy, violent, dishonest man who gambled and drank too much; when he was convicted of stealing money, he was sent to prison and his family's home was taken from them. At that point, Gibran's mother decided to take her children to the United States.

Gibran knew that he could write in a way that touched people's hearts. He made himself a spokesperson not only for the Syrian people, but also for all people regardless of their race or religion. His book *The Prophet* (1923) is the second best-selling book in America in the twentieth century (behind the Bible); it has been translated into twenty languages and is popular around the world.

Kahlil Gibran. *Reproduced by permission of Corbis Corporation (Bellevue).*

You is the only golden chain that
Binds your rich heart to the
Loving heart of God. . . .

(*Gibran,* Secrets of the Heart, *pp. 92–93, 96*)

What happened next . . .

World War I ended with the defeat of the Turkish Ottoman Empire and its allies (friendly nations). Syria and

Lebanon were divided into separate countries, both of which were under the control of France. During the 1940s, France's involvement in World War II left it unable to govern Syria and Lebanon; it withdrew and the countries became independent.

Did you know . . .

• Gibran encouraged other men to join the French army and drive Turkish rule out of Syria. He himself was unable to join because a childhood accident had permanently damaged his left shoulder.

• Gibran's urgings for the Lebanese people to revolt against the Turks angered people who supported that government. He received threatening letters and was even wounded in an assassination attempt.

For More Information

Gibran, Jean, and Kahlil Gibran. *Kahlil Gibran, His Life and World,* rev. ed. Brooklyn, NY: Interlink, 1991.

Gibran, Kahlil. "Dead Are My People." *Secrets of the Heart,* translated by Anthony Rizcallah Ferris. New York: Signet Books, 1947, pp. 92–96.

Salom Rizk

Syrian Yankee
**Excerpt from the autobiography of Salom Rizk
Published in 1943**

Salom Rizk (1909–1973) was born an American citizen. His parents immigrated to the United States and became citizens before he was born. He did not discover this, however, until he was twelve years old. When he was born his mother was visiting relatives in Syria. She died giving birth to him. Rizk's grandmother, a lonely but loving woman whose sons had all left Syria, raised him until she died. Rizk, who was then seven, walked by himself to another village in search of his other grandmother. On the way, he crossed a field where a battle had recently been fought in World War I (1914–18); it was strewn with rotting corpses—a horrific sight that haunted him throughout his life.

Several years later, a teacher who had befriended Rizk searched for information about his parents and found out that his father and brothers were living in America. His family sent money for Rizk to buy a ticket on a ship that would bring him to them. But it took five years to prove to the U.S. government that he was really the son of American citizens; births were not officially recorded in small Syrian villages like the one in which he was born. He finally received permission

"I knew that I was living proof to them of what America was and what America could be."

A view of Talbeseh, a mud-house village typical of northern Syria. *Reproduced by permission of AP/Wide World Photos.*

to come to the United States in 1927. After docking in New York City, he took a train to Sioux City, Iowa, where he met his brothers. His father had died before he arrived.

Rizk's experience was unique: born an American citizen, he was treated as a foreigner when he came "home" to the United States. Yet his experience was like that of innumerable other immigrants: he struggled to learn English, he adapted to an extraordinarily different culture, and he worked to support himself so he would not be a burden on anyone else.

Things to remember while reading the excerpt from *Syrian Yankee:*

- Rizk describes several of the reasons for the first wave of Middle Eastern immigration to the United States: economic hardship (like that caused by crop failures), devastation caused by World War I, and the harsh rule of the Turkish Ottoman Empire.

- Rizk was eighteen years old when he came to the United States. His brothers gave him the American nickname "Sam." He was twenty when he decided to take classes in a public school so he could become fluent in English. He was placed in a fourth grade class, where he gave his first speech.

- Rizk's speech was so popular that other teachers invited him to talk to their classes. Soon he was invited to speak at a luncheon meeting of the local Rotary Club.

Syrian Yankee

[In Syria]

*The first wave of the war to flow over and around us was the **refugees** from the Lebanon. They poured over the hills, through the narrow passes, and down the valleys—men, women, and children by the hundreds, fleeing from the wrath that had come. They came with inconsolable grief in their hearts, with horror in their eyes and the sag of weariness in their thin faces. . . .*

They told how their children had been murdered in cold blood before their very eyes, and their fathers and mothers, too, who were too old to flee. They told of whole villages evacuated, looted, burned and destroyed. . . .

*In the meantime, we were visited by two kinds of **plagues**: one of locusts, the other of men, and of the two the latter was the worse. The locusts came in summer. . . . They came—by the billions—and they darkened the skies and filled the air with a great whirring of wings. It really frightened me. They fell on everything, the fields and fig trees, the vineyards and the pastures, until every inch of earth was crawling black with them, and yet the sky was full of them. They devoured everything they touched, the bark of trees, the feathers of chickens, and the hair of goats. . . .*

*After they were gone there were sadness and **foreboding** in the valley, and the sadness was for what the locusts had done and the foreboding was for what the tax collectors would do.*

Refugees: People who leave their homes to escape war or political upheaval.

Plague: A widespread disaster caused by disease or natural elements.

Foreboding: Fear of what is to come.

*They came, the tax collectors did, in the time of harvest. They stayed in our houses as if they owned them. They watched every move we made **lest** we steal our own wheat from under their noses. When the wheat was piled by our houses—in small piles outdoors, for there was not much because of the locusts—they placed the great seal of the Turkish government on the wheat and went to bed—on our mats. If the seal was broken in the morning, it was the owner who suffered. So every owner and the members of his family lived in fear of the seal being broken. They stayed up all night and took turns guarding the wheat piles against thieves and stray dogs and cats and anything else that might break the soft seal on the wheat. Those were the days when even the wind was feared because it could blow up strong and break the great seal, too; but since you cannot catch the wind to punish it, you simply catch the owner and punish him. . . .*

*The tax gatherers did not fail to come, again and again, raiding the village systematically, house by house, room by room, person by person. Nothing was too small or insignificant or useless-looking for them to seize. Every scrap of metal, even down to the tiny iron points on the wooden plows, was carted off to feed the **insatiable** war machine. When they started to empty the feathers out of our pillows to make sandbags, my aunt Zarefy was ready to fight. But there was really nothing one could do. . . .*

*The men also resisted military service. Not that they were cowards. They would gladly have fought for a cause they believed in. But they did not believe in the cause of being **oppressed** by the Turks or by anyone else. So some of the men mutilated themselves—cut off their fingers, broke their arms, or poured scalding water on their feet. Others hid out in the hills. . . .*

[In America]

It is hard to describe the mixture of feelings I had the day I was to speak to the Rotarians. . . . [One of the leaders told me] Rotary was international, a club for businessmen in all the nations, an organization standing for service and good will and peace and fair play for all, everywhere in the world.

*With that everything went flat inside of me. I felt insignificant and ashamed, **assailed** with doubts about my appearing here. Why should I speak to these people? What could I say to them that they did not already know, that any one of them could not say better than I could? . . .*

Lest: Fearing.

Insatiable: Unable to be satisfied.

Oppressed: Downtrodden; spiritually broken.

Assailed: Attacked.

Something was wrong with my stomach, and my heart was racing like a windmill.

When Dr. Helser said, "I am happy to present Sam Rizk, an American who had to discover his own country," I struggled to my feet and looked blankly in front of me. For a moment that seemed endless my memory was a complete emptiness, and the blur of faces and eyes and clapping hands before me resembled a nightmare.

Then I remembered what I wanted to say.

"Ladies and gentlemen," I started, and I was suddenly terrified by the thickness of my accent. "Please do not think that I am a speaker. I am not a speaker. I am only a dishwater. I mean, I mean, I am only a dishwasher."

*Well, everybody laughed so hard I began to wonder if they were ever going to stop. But after that everything became easy. The friendliest thing in the world is a laugh, even when it is at your own expense. I forgot my prepared speech and told my story just the way I had told it to the kids in school: How I was born in Syria and my mother died, leaving me to be cared for by a grandmother. How the death of my grandmother left me a miserable and ragged orphan in war-torn Syria. How I managed to survive by eating raw birds' eggs and roots in the hills. How I learned I was an American citizen. How it took five long, painful years to prove it. How at last I came to America, and how I felt when I saw this vast, rich land with its great farms and **teeming** cities. . . . How I appreciated the privileges and opportunities of this great and miraculous land, the friendliness and helpfulness of its people. . . .*

When I got through, I sat down and everybody else stood up. They applauded and applauded until Mr. Davis motioned me to stand up, too. I knew they were not applauding me. They were applauding America, the land where something like this could happen to anybody, a land where a man was free, with the help of his fellows, to work out his own destiny. I knew that I was living proof to them of what America was and what America could be. They were proud of a nation because of me. But I could not feel proud. It was a very great and a very humbling experience. (Rizk, Syrian Yankee, pp. 36–41, 189, 191–94)

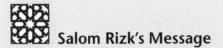

Salom Rizk's Message

For twenty years, Salom Rizk (1909–1973) traveled around the United States giving speeches about what it means to be an American. In his autobiography, *Syrian Yankee,* he explained why he wanted so much to deliver this message:

> During this first year in school came one of my greatest astonishments: that Americans—especially young school-going Americans—took their many blessings and opportunities so much for granted. That everybody could speak and write and worship as he pleased did not seem strange to anybody. That education was free for everyone down to the humblest of citizens amazed no one. In Ain Arab [Syria] I used to long for just one sheet of paper to write on. I hungered for just one book to read, one book to call my own, and I used to rescue scraps of Syrian newspaper from the gutters of Beirut, take them home, and feast on them a whole evening. But here in America books and papers were everywhere, the schools were as magnificent as palaces. . . . How could anyone take all this grand achievement for granted? (Rizk, p. 177)

What happened next . . .

After speaking to the Rotary Club, Rizk began to speak to other civic organizations. His passion for spreading his message became so great that he sold his shoe repair business and began traveling around the eastern United States giving speeches for a fee. After four years of living in a run-down car while he drove from speech to speech, Rizk was invited to speak at the New York City Advertising Club in 1939. In the audience were representatives of the Readers Digest Association who were so impressed with his speech that they hired him to tour the entire country and talk to high school students. German dictator Adolph Hitler (1889–1945) had invaded neighboring Austria in 1938. The next three years, which coincided with Rizk's speaking tour, saw World War II (1939–45) get under way. More than one million students heard Rizk's patriotic message, which helped inspire young Americans at a critical time.

Did you know . . .

- Before becoming a professional speaker, Rizk owned a shoe repair shop. During the Great Depression (1929–40; a time when many businesses failed and one-fourth of American workers could not find jobs), Rizk collected worn-out shoes, repaired them, and gave them to the poor.

- Word of Rizk's "shoes for the poor" program spread, and he was invited to speak at the National Shoe Dealers convention in Chicago, Illinois. Soon more than three hundred shops in the United States and Canada were performing free shoe repairs for unemployed people.

- Rizk died at his home in Maryland in 1973 at the age of sixty-three. The *New York Times* published a several-paragraph obituary describing his patriotic speaking career.

For More Information

Hall, Loretta, and Bridget K. Hall. "Salom Rizk." *Arab American Biography.* Farmington Hills, MI: U•X•L, 1999.

Rizk, Salom. *Syrian Yankee.* Garden City, NY: Doubleday, 1943.

Hannah Sabbagh Shakir

"Hannah Sabbagh Shakir"
Selection from *Bint Arab: Arab and Arab American Women in the United States,* by Evelyn Shakir Published in 1997

Hannah Sabbagh Shakir (1895–1990) emigrated from Lebanon to the United States in 1907 at the age of twelve. In Lebanon, few women worked outside the home; their role was primarily to raise children, cook, and take care of other household responsibilities like feeding animals and tending vegetable gardens. Syrian women who immigrated to America often worked outside the home, however.

Peddling (selling merchandise door-to-door or on the street) and working in factories were the most common occupations for first-wave Syrian immigrants. Many factories, trying to increase their profits, treated their workers badly, providing low pay and dangerous or unpleasant working conditions. Labor unions organized workers to demand better treatment by threatening to go on strike (stop working) if their demands were not met. Particularly in Michigan's automobile plants and in New England's textile and garment factories, Syrian workers took an active part in these labor disputes.

In the Lebanese culture, it was considered very important to operate one's own business, rather than work for someone else. Like Shakir, many Lebanese immigrants saved enough

"I was very embarrassed. How could I walk in a picket line! There was a very spirited woman I worked with. 'Well,' she said to me, 'do you want someone else to fight your fight for you?' We lost that time, and I lost my job."

money from peddling or other jobs to start their own businesses such as dry goods stores, bakeries, or small factories (especially in the garment industry).

Things to remember while reading "Hannah Sabbagh Shakir":

- Shakir had five brothers: Elias, Rashid, Alexander, Litfallah, and Naseeb; only Naseeb was younger than she.

- It is not clear why Shakir's father was not working after they moved to Fall River, Massachusetts. But, as reported in *Bint Arab,* the fourteen-year-old girl "felt betrayed by Litfallah, the brother . . . to whom—until he shrugged his responsibilities onto her shoulders—she had felt the closest."

- Because of their experiences with the tyrannical Turkish government in their homeland, Syrian immigrants were afraid to complain to governmental officials in America about things like poor working conditions.

"Hannah Sabbagh Shakir"

A young girl stands in front of a power loom in a textile factory. Peddling and working in factories were the most common occupations for first-wave Syrian immigrants. Workers often went on strike to protest poor working conditions and long hours.

When we moved to Fall River, I didn't go to school any more. I had to work. My mother and father weren't working. Rashid had gotten married and left us. Elias was working as a salesman in the South. Alexander had learned to weave, but he didn't work much. Litfallah had learned, too, and when we went to Fall River he taught me. I was fourteen then. After three or four weeks, when he saw I could handle to job, he quit. He gave me his job and left. Then he got married and moved back to Boston. So I had to make money for the rest of us to live on. . . .

*I worked in the biggest **textile** mill in Fall River. We made **gingham**. I learned how to operate the looms, six big looms, just like a man. I did it very well. The looms ran by themselves, but when one stopped, I'd go and examine it to see what was wrong. If a thread was broken, I'd rethread it. If the spool was empty, I'd replace it. Some days luck was bad, the machines would keep breaking down, the threads would keep snapping, and you had to undo the damaged sections. Other days everything went smoothly.*

But it was hard work. When I first started, we used to work twelve hours a day, from six in the morning til six at night. And on Saturdays, til twelve. . . .

*I began working as a stitcher in a big Boston factory. That was about 1925. I worked in a **union** shop, we paid 10 cents a week dues.*

*Once they called a big union meeting of people from all the shops. We met in a big hall and listened to speeches. One man was a very skillful speaker. "A man works his whole life away! He shouldn't have to kill himself! He should get a good living!" So we **went out on strike.** I thought we could just stay home. But no, we had to go in every day and walk in the **picket line.** I was very embarrassed. How could I walk in a picket line! There was a very spirited woman I worked with. "Well," she said to me, "do you want someone else to fight your fight for you?" We lost that time, and I lost my job.*

*Another time there was a big strike [in March 1936]. . . . Police came on horseback and held the strikers back so the **strike-breakers** could go in. Sometimes the strikers would stop them as they left work and talk to them. "Why are you doing this? This is our bread and butter we're fighting for!" Sometimes they would beat up the strike-breakers.*

The union was very good in some ways. If a girl had worked in a place for a long time and decided to go to the old country, let's say for a year, when she came back, the boss had to give her back her old machine. . . . And when you first started a job, if the boss didn't like your work, he could fire you. But if you worked several weeks, then he couldn't fire you no matter what. . . . So you were sure of your job. (Hannah Sabbagh Shakir in Bint Arab, pp. 47, 50)

Textile: Fabric.

Gingham: A plain-weave cotton fabric made of died thread, usually in a striped or checkered pattern.

Union: An organization of workers who unite to bargain with their employers for better pay and working conditions.

Went out on strike: To refuse to work in the hopes that an employer will give in to striker demands for better working conditions or better pay; employers don't profit if their shops are shut down.

Picket line: A line of striking workers who are protesting their treatment by their employer.

Strike-breakers: People who are hired to work in place of employees who are on strike.

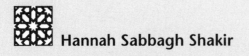

Hannah Sabbagh Shakir

Hannah Sabbagh Shakir was born in 1895 in a tiny village in the mountains of Lebanon. Three of her older brothers immigrated to the United States, and when Shakir was about ten years old, her mother left to visit them. When she finally returned after a year, she convinced her husband that they and their three youngest children must also move to Boston, Massachusetts.

After Shakir began working in factories, she was too busy to be interested in getting married. Although she had several proposals over the years, she did not marry until she was thirty-six years old. Her husband, Wadie Shakir, owned a one-man printing company. After their daughter and son were born, Hannah Shakir continued working in factories, and her mother cared for the children during working hours. When she was seventy-one, Shakir retired. She died in 1990 at the age of ninety-five.

What happened next . . .

At the age of fifty, Hannah Shakir started her own business, a sportswear factory, in suburban Boston, Massachusetts. Her daughter, Evelyn Shakir, who was in the fifth grade when her mother opened her factory, saw that the work was hard: "By the end of the day, the women's backs would ache, and their eyesight would blur. In summer, fuzz from the wool they were working on—they were always one season ahead—would coat their sweaty faces and arms." But Hannah Shakir had seen firsthand the improvements labor unions won in working conditions, workday length, and fair pay. She respected her employees' needs and treated them as friends. Her daughter wrote, "If they had small children in school, Hannah let them go home when school let out; if they needed money, she lent them small sums, interest-free." (Evelyn Shakir in *Bint Arab*, pp. 47, 50)

Did you know . . .

- Shakir came to America in 1907, in the middle of a fifteen-year period during which nearly one-half of the Arab immigrants were women. Before 1900, most Syrian immigrants were men who came alone, often leaving their families behind while they worked to earn more money than they could in Lebanon.

- At the time Shakir came to America, one-fourth of the Syrian immigrants returned to their homeland after a few years; however, most of them eventually came back, often with their families.

- Shakir learned to read and write English at her school in Lebanon, but her spoken English was not good when she

Syrian Involvement in the Bread and Roses Strike

The labor strikes Hannah Shakir described were not unusual. One of the most famous strikes against textile mills took place in Lawrence, Massachusetts, in 1912. A new state law went into effect saying women and children could work no more than fifty-four hours a week (sixty-six was customary). Factories complied but refused to raise the hourly wage; as a result, family incomes decreased significantly. Twenty thousand workers, mostly women and children, went on strike for sixty-three days. Their slogan, "We want bread and roses too," noted that they demanded more pleasant working conditions as well as better pay.

Led by a half-Syrian organizer from the Industrial Workers of the World (IWW) union, the strike was a difficult ordeal. A Boston librarian who researched the strike eighty years later wrote:

> During a bitter cold spell and a swirling snowstorm, between seven and eight thousand strikers had formed a picket line around the mills to keep others from entering. There were militiamen with bayonets and policemen with firehoses. The strikers never forgot the icy blasts from the firehoses. There was an accidental stabbing of a Syrian boy—John Rami—a sixteen year old innocent bystander.
>
> He was killed when the militia pushed the strikers with bayonets to get them to move on. . . .
>
> The strike showed the importance of ethnic organizations in the life of that city during the strike. The Syrian band, meetings beneath the Syrian Church, the Syrian relief work, and the Syrian soup kitchens are examples.
>
> In the Syrian soup kitchens, women prepared the food while the men assisted in serving at the long tables. They fed from 140 to 150 twice a day during the strike. A typical menu was bread, lamb, crushed wheat (burghul), specially prepared cultured milk (laban), and coffee. Another meal consisted of bread, rice, lima bean stew (yakhnit fasoolya), and coffee. (Menconi, pp. 46–49)

The strike resulted in pay raises for the workers, not only at the factories that were struck, but in other nearby industries as well.

first came to America. When she started school in Boston at age twelve, she was placed in a first-grade class, but she quickly progressed to classes closer to her age group.

For More Information

Menconi, Evelyn Abdalah, ed. *The Coffeehouse Wayn Ma Kan Collection: Memories of the Syrian-Lebanese Community of Boston.* Boston: William G. Abdalah Memorial Library, 1996.

Shakir, Evelyn. *Bint Arab: Arab and Arab American Women in the United States.* Westport, CT: Praeger, 1997.

Gladys Shibley Sadd

"First Generation Americans:
The Bridge between Yesterday and Tomorrow"

Selection from a speech to the Boston Arab American community
Delivered October 11, 1982
Published in 1996 in *The Coffeehouse Wayn Ma Kan Collection*,
edited by Evelyn Abdalah Menconi

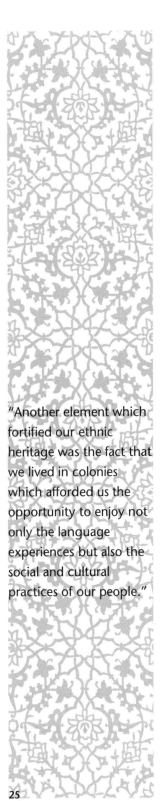

"Another element which fortified our ethnic heritage was the fact that we lived in colonies which afforded us the opportunity to enjoy not only the language experiences but also the social and cultural practices of our people."

G ladys Shibley Sadd grew up in three Syrian communities in Boston, Massachusetts. Both of her parents had immigrated to the United States from Lebanon about 1890. They married in 1902 and began to raise their family in the original Syrian colony near the harbor in downtown Boston. After about ten years, they joined several other Syrian families in establishing a second Boston-area Syrian community in what was then a rustic suburb called West Roxbury. During World War I (1914–18), the family moved back into the city to be closer to the war materials factory where Sadd's father worked. By that time, a new Syrian community had become established in the downtown area. Within each of these ethnic communities, Arab Americans could find restaurants and grocery stores with their favorite foods, people with similar customs and values, and churches (Christian places of worship) and mosques (Muslim places of worship) where they could practice their traditional religion.

Nearly seventy years after the war, on October 11, 1982, Sadd was invited to talk about her childhood experiences at a program sponsored by the Boston Arab American community. She told the audience, "I feel especially fortunate

A group of Syrian children in New York City, c. 1908–15.

Reproduced by permission of Corbis Corporation (Bellevue).

to be a first generation American because it was my generation which enjoyed the unadulterated [pure] values of our parental culture." A written version of the speech was published in *The Coffeehouse Wayn Ma Kan Collection: Memories of the Syrian-Lebanese Community of Boston* in 1996.

Things to remember while reading the selection from "First Generation Americans: The Bridge between Yesterday and Tomorrow":

- First-generation Americans are people who were born in the United States but whose parents came from other countries.

- Sadd's father was from the Lebanese village of Shleefa, and her mother was from the village of Duma. Before coming to America at the age of nineteen, Sadd's father had worked as a caravaneer, escorting travelers and merchants from one city to another. These birthplace and job associations eventually formed the basis for clubs organized in the Boston Syrian community.

- *Arabian Nights* is a collection of ancient Arabic folktales that were first gathered together about the year 1000. Around the 1400s they were organized within a unifying plot: a wife, Sheherazade, keeps her husband, a legendary king, entertained by telling him a story every night for 1,001 nights so he wouldn't execute her. Ali Baba and the forty thieves, Aladdin and the magical lamp, and the adventures of Sinbad the Sailor are only a few of the stories of the *Arabian Nights*. Even though they are fictional, the tales contain many details of traditional life in the Middle East.

"First Generation Americans: The Bridge between Yesterday and Tomorrow"

*We spoke Arabic at home so as very young children we were **bilingual**. As a result of this early exposure to Arabic and its beautiful expressions and **proverbs**, I have had a life-long affair with what I consider the most beautiful language in the world. . . .*

*Another element which **fortified** our ethnic heritage was the fact that we lived in colonies which afforded us the opportunity to enjoy not only the language experiences but also the social and cultural practices of our people (such as Haflis [parties], the music and dances at the Sahras [celebrations] and the rawayat—or drama—which depicted social customs, **amateurish** and educational and entertaining).*

At the turn of the [twentieth] century, our first Syrian colony or community was the Hudson Street colony; boundaries were Essex Street on the North, Broadway on the South, Albany Street to the East and Harrison Avenue to the West. There were "papa" operated grocery stores, bakeries, coffeehouses, dry goods stores, sweets shops, and the Church at 32 Hudson Street. The second colony— West Roxbury—shortly before World War I (1911–15) several adventurous families migrated to a sparsely populated suburb called West Roxbury. . . .

Bilingual: Able to speak two languages.

Proverbs: Wise sayings.

Fortified: Strengthened.

Amateurish: Nonprofessional.

The most important factor in our ethnic development was the family unit. In those days there was no T.V., no radio, so on the long winter evenings mother entertained us children by telling us stories about Jehhy, Ioz Zeer and Arabian Nights in Arabic. These were the things which served to formulate and fortify both our ethnic values and the family unit. . . .

Saturday in West Roxbury was "Happy Day." First, it was baking day when mother did the baking for the week. Baking beans in the bean pot, the air hung heavy with the **tantalizing** *aroma of baking beans. The bean pot was placed in the back of the oven while the bread baked—since it took all day to bake the beans. We could hardly wait for the first loaf to come out of the oven so that we could enjoy a slice of bread with butter, yum! Supper of course would be the traditional baked beans, frankforts, and cole slaw. . . .*

Our parents had an **inordinate** *reverence for learning. Because of their lack of formal education, they encouraged us to achieve academically and experienced* **vicariously** *great joy and pride in our academic successes. Our parents made every effort to learn English and encouraged us to help them. I can remember my Mom and so many of the neighbors going to night classes at the Franklin School to learn English. We first-generation Americans, both boys and girls, were academically goal-oriented. Most of us knew when we entered high school what professions we wanted to pursue. . . .*

Besides the ethnic factors, the most important of which I consider the home, there were numerous institutions instrumental in our development. Our churches, for the most part, played a **negligible** *role in this area because our priests, who spoke little English, functioned on Sunday only. However, we benefitted greatly from our schools, libraries, community centers. Denison House served Hudson Street colony: clubs for children, summer camping programs, meeting place for youth groups. . . . Morgan Memorial [Chapel] served both Hudson Street and Shawmut Avenue colonies: Sunday School, church services, church socials, camping programs, vacation school activities, book stores. South End House served Shawmut Avenue colony: mother's club, weekly meetings, monthly luncheons, camping program for mothers. Others included the Syrian Educational Society about 1920—a philanthropic scholarship to worthy students; Middle East Relief—early 1900s sent money to Lebanon—disaster relief and poor villages; Syrian-Lebanese Ladies' Aid started in 1917—charity* **discreetly**, *scholarships, still active; Child Welfare Society—late 1920s (of which I am a charter member)—raised money*

Tantalizing: Tempting.

Inordinate: Extreme.

Vicariously: Through the experience of another person.

Negligible: Very small, unimportant.

Discreetly: Quietly; hidden.

to send children to camp, bought our own camp Hammond from BYMCU, first Syrian-owned in U.S. The Caravaneers—about 1929–30—college men and women primarily social, drama and debates, drew large community audiences. . . .

*Our chief contribution to the Syrian community was to inspire the tomorrow generation to keep the faith and strive for academic excellence. There were village **benevolent** societies: the Duma Society, the Shleefa Society, etc.; the Eastern Federation of Clubs (organized here in Boston about 1932). This organization marked the awakening of ethnic unity and the beginning of **Pan-Arabism**. (Sadd in Menconi, pp. 14–17)*

What happened next . . .

Various Arab groups are no more alike in history and culture than English-speaking people from America, Australia, Britain, and India. The Pan-Arabism Sadd mentioned was a movement to unify all Arab people by emphasizing the common aspects of their language and customs rather than their national differences. Especially through the efforts of Egyptian President Gamal Abdal Nasser (1918–1970), Pan-Arabism became a political movement to unite the Arab nations in opposition to the nation of Israel, which was established in 1948 on land that had belonged to Palestinian Arabs. From 1958 until 1961, Egypt, Syria, and Yemen even joined into a single country, called the United Arab Republic. Israel's defeat of Egyptian and Syrian armies in 1967 during the Six Day War brought Nasser's Pan-Arabism to an end. On another level, modern organizations like the American-Arab Anti-Discrimination Committee (ADC) and the Association of Arab-American University Graduates (AAUG) welcome Arab Americans regardless of their country of origin.

Did you know . . .

- During the early 1900s, Boston had about 3,000 Syrian residents. By 1955, the number had increased to about 11,000.

Benevolent: Charitable.

Pan-Arabism: The movement to unify all the Arab nations of the Middle East so that, as a group, they have more power in world politics.

Arab American Relief Efforts

Arab Americans tend to live in clusters, preserving their ethnic heritage and offering one another emotional, spiritual, and material support. Often these communities are centered around churches or mosques. Various groups have also formed cultural, professional, business, and political organizations. Often these groups undertake projects to help not only the Arab immigrant community but also suffering people in the Middle East.

For example, two civil wars were being fought in Iraq in 1991—one in the northern part of the country and one in the southern part. Both wars involved rival Muslim groups. Only about 3 percent of Iraqis are Christian, and these people were exposed to the civil wars without protection from any of the Muslim groups. In 1993, a group of Chaldean (Roman Catholic Iraqi) Americans from Michigan went to Washington, D.C., to ask permission for 20,000 Christian refugees from Iraq to enter the United States. The 60,000-member Chaldean community of Detroit promised its financial and emotional support to the refugees if they were allowed to come to America.

Arab American groups around the country have arranged to bring children injured in the ongoing Palestinian–Israeli conflict to the United States for medical treatment. In one case, the Arab community of Albuquerque, New Mexico, brought a ten-year-old boy named Nidal to America for treatment of a bullet wound. Jamil Toubbeh, a member of the sponsoring group, described the boy's injury from being shot with a so-called "rubber" bullet: "Nidal . . . was hit by one that penetrated his pelvic region, causing severe damage to his large colon and peripheral nervous system. The exit wound was three inches in diameter." The New Mexico Arab Americans provided emotional support for the boy in addition to travel expenses and medical treatment.

- The first major Syrian American communities developed in the port cities of Boston; New York, New York; and Philadelphia, Pennsylvania, where many of the immigrants entered the United States. Between 1910 and 1930, more than 5,000 Syrian Americans moved to Detroit, Michigan, where they found jobs in automobile factories and related industries. By 1980, the Detroit area had the country's largest Arab American population—more than 200,000.

- The Syrian Ladies' Aid Society of Boston was founded in 1917 to send relief supplies to Syria, which was being devastated by World War I and by crop failures. After the war ended, the society turned its attention to helping poor Syrian Americans living in Boston.

For More Information

Sadd, Gladys Shibley. "First Generation Americans: The Bridge between Yesterday and Tomorrow." *The Coffeehouse Wayn Ma Kan Collection: Memories of the Syrian-Lebanese Community of Boston,* edited by Evelyn Abdalah Menconi. Boston: William G. Abdalah Memorial Library, 1996.

Shakir, Evelyn. *Bint Arab: Arab and Arab American Women in the United States.* Westport, CT: Praeger, 1997, pp. 59–64.

Joseph J. Jacobs

The Anatomy of an Entrepreneur
Excerpt from the autobiography of Joseph J. Jacobs
Published in 1991

W hen he was growing up in Brooklyn during the 1920s, Joseph J. Jacobs (1916–) was one of about 5,000 Syrian Americans living in New York City (Brooklyn is a borough, or county, of New York City). Like other immigrant groups, the Syrian Americans formed their own community in which they could associate with other people who spoke the same native language, ate the same types of foods, and shared the same cultural values and customs. During the late 1800s, the New York Syrian community developed along Washington Street in lower Manhattan (another borough). As the Syrian businesses prospered, virtually the entire community moved to Brooklyn Heights. After World War I (1914–18), many of the Syrians, including Jacobs's family, relocated to a fashionable Brooklyn neighborhood called Park Slope.

In his autobiography, *The Anatomy of an Entrepreneur,* and in other articles and speeches, Jacobs described his community in two ways that seem almost opposite. On the one hand, the Syrian Americans found safety and comfort in staying close to their fellow Syrians, considering themselves one

"Our parents wanted us to be Americans, but not at the expense of our own heritage."

A Syrian-Lebanese immigrant toting an ornate metal container full of water sells cool drinks in the Syrian quarter of New York City, c. 1900. *Reproduced by permission of Corbis Corporation (Bellevue).*

large family. In Jacobs's words, all the Lebanese in New York City thought of themselves as "cousins." (Because Lebanon was a region of Syria at the time, an immigrant from Lebanon might be called either Lebanese or Syrian.)

On the other hand, the New York Syrian colony was larger and more diverse than most immigrant communities. Although they had come from the same country—Greater Syria—these immigrants considered their affiliations with thirteen different tribes to be more important than their shared Lebanese nationality. "Leaderless in many ways," Arab historian Philip Hitti wrote in 1924, "yet deluged with petty and self-made leaders, Syrians in [the United States] present a lamentable sight." Jacobs, fortunately, held an opposing view. "When I visited Lebanon [around 1980], I saw the destructive potential of multiculturalism," he wrote in *American Enterprise* magazine. "I had seen hints of it among the Lebanese in Brooklyn, but the overwhelming sense of being American made tribal rivalries trivial."

The feeling of ethnic identity and community support Jacobs experienced as a Lebanese American was far stronger than the rivalries. Reflecting on his life, he wrote in *The Anatomy of an Entrepreneur,* "It is clear that the influences that determined my values and helped me become [a successful businessman] came, not only out of my immediate family, but also out of the entire ethnic community in which I was raised."

Things to remember while reading the excerpt from *The Anatomy of an Entrepreneur:*

- An entrepreneur is a person who starts a business and assumes personal responsibility for the success or failure of the company. Like Jacobs's father, most Syrian immigrants became entrepreneurs, starting retail businesses with the money they saved while working as independent peddlers (door-to-door salespeople). Jacobs became a chemical engineer, and after working for a large chemical company for a few years, he started his own engineering company. The company has been extraordinarily successful; in 1997 it had nearly 16,000 employees.

- The Maronite Church is part of the Roman Catholic Church, which recognizes the pope as its leader. The Eastern Orthodox Church separated from the Roman Catholic church in 1054; the worldwide leader of the Eastern Orthodox Church is the Patriarch of Antioch. (The city of Antioch, now called Antakya, was in Syria from 1918 until 1939, when it became part of Turkey.)

- Jacobs married Violet "Vi" Jabara in 1942, the day after his twenty-sixth birthday. She was also a Lebanese American, but she was not a Maronite Catholic like Jacobs was. At that time, a wedding between a Catholic and a non-Catholic could not be performed inside a church. Even though they were married in the less sacred atmosphere of a private home, the Jacobses' wedding was an elaborate, joyful affair full of religious symbolism.

The Anatomy of an Entrepreneur

[Childhood]

*Our parents wanted us to be Americans, but not at the expense of our own heritage. They distinguished so sharply between the two cultures that they developed an almost **dualistic** outlook.*

*Americans were different, they were outside the tribe. Most of the ethnic immigrants, the Italians, Poles, Germans, Scandinavians, and others, tended to live in **enclaves** where the mother tongue was the everyday language and English was kept primarily for **commerce** with Americans. So did the Lebanese.*

As all families do, we squabbled. Even in Brooklyn we had time for tribal and religious differences. Most of the Lebanese we knew were Christians, either Maronite or Eastern Orthodox. Between these two only slightly differing churches there was a pronounced rivalry that was a pale reflection of the ancient tribal feuds that have virtually destroyed Lebanon today. . . .

[About 1923]

Often on Saturdays, when I was about six or seven, [my father] would take me by streetcar to the office for half a day's work, to look at the mail, and then we would go on to the Washington Market in lower Manhattan. The farmers brought their produce to a large warehouse building and the brokers or wholesalers and the grocery store owners of the city would come in at 4 or 5 A.M. to pick over the offerings and buy their fresh produce for the day.

*The market was an exotic place where one could buy all sorts of unusual delicacies, such as squid and sea urchins, those spiny, hard-shelled mollusks whose orange flesh my father enjoyed, and rare fruit, such as prickly pears, the fruit of a cactus, that had to be washed and scrubbed while one wore thick gloves to avoid the spines. Then we would cut the skin and savor the sweet, cold flesh. Stalls in the building catered to retail customers who bought fruit and vegetables by the case and, with each box of figs or apricots he bought, my father would **regale** me with his exaggerated memories of the superior fruit in Lebanon. These were great outings for me, for I had Pop to myself for a whole morning. In a family of seven children, those were times to be cherished. I played with the typewriter*

Dualistic: Divided into two separate parts.

Enclaves: Separate ethnic communities.

Commerce: Business transactions.

Regale: Entertain.

in his office, scribbled on his note pads, and went home happy in the open-air streetcar, weighed down with cases of fruit, unusual meats, and all the Middle Eastern ingredients Mom needed to cook her marvelous meals. . . .

[His 1942 marriage]

The cultural pressures, especially when exerted by my mother, were strong indeed. Father Stephen agreed to marry us in [Vi's] house, since we were not allowed to be married in church. The Maronite ritual is full of symbolism that is mostly beyond my knowledge, but I do recall that orange blossom crowns were placed upon our heads. They symbolized that we were the "king" and "queen" of a new family to be formed. During the ceremony the crowns were passed back and forth between us three times to denote the interchangeability of our **dominion** *over our future family. The ritual was colorful and impressive, with its chanting and incense and ancient* **Aramaic** *prayers. (Jacobs,* Anatomy, *pp. 20, 23, 76)*

What happened next . . .

The New York colony was the first large Syrian American community; it was also the most culturally diverse and the most economically successful of the early Arab American communities. It became an intellectual center for Middle Eastern immigrants. Prominent Syrian authors, poets, and philosophers like **Kahlil Gibran**, Ameen Rihany, and Michail Naimy gathered there, and in 1920 they formed the Pen League to promote modern styles of writing in Arabic. By 1928, six Arabic-language daily newspapers were being printed in New York City; each represented a segment of the Syrian community, such as the Maronite Catholics, the Eastern Orthodox Christians, or the Druze (an Islamic sect).

Did you know . . .

- Approximately 12 percent of Arab Americans own their own businesses, compared to 7 percent of all Americans.

Dominion: Authority.

Aramaic: (air-eh-MAY-ic) an ancient Semitic language.

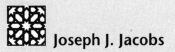

Joseph J. Jacobs

Joseph J. Jacobs's mother emigrated from Lebanon with her parents when she was nine years old. Jacobs's father, who was also Lebanese, came to the United States by himself in 1886 at the age of sixteen. He worked as a peddler for many years, settling down and opening a store in Brooklyn shortly before his seventh child was born. Joseph Jacobs was that youngest child.

At times, the family was wealthy, but at other times business was not good and they struggled financially. When Jacobs was twelve years old, he got his first job, selling soft drinks and snacks at a stand in Prospect Park in Brooklyn, New York. During the summer, he worked twelve hours a day to help support his family. When Jacobs was sixteen, his father died. When Jacobs started college, he had to keep earning money, so he worked six hours a day while he was going to school.

Jacobs continued his education until he earned a Ph.D. (doctorate) in chemical engineering in 1942. World War II (1939–45) was raging at the time, but Jacobs could not serve in the military because his eyesight was too poor. Instead, he went to work for a large chemical company, where he invented a process for mass-producing penicillin, a new antibiotic that saved thousands of soldiers' lives.

In 1947, with the war over, Jacobs started his own engineering company, which is now called the Jacobs Engineering Group. One of the firm's largest projects was a potash refinery it designed and built in Jordan. The plant, which took twenty years to build and cost $450 million, was completed in 1982. While working on the potash plant, Jacobs traveled to the Middle East and met his Lebanese relatives.

- In 1990, 80 percent of Arab Americans at least sixteen years old had a job, compared to 60 percent of the same age group of all Americans.

- In 1990, the median (average) annual income of Arab American families was $39,100. The median income for all American families was only $30,100.

For More Information

El-Badry, Samia. "The Arab-American Market." *American Demographics,* January 1994.

Hitti, Philip. *The Syrians in America*. New York: George H. Doran, 1924.

Jacobs, Joseph J. *The Anatomy of an Entrepreneur*. San Francisco: ICS Press, 1991.

Jacobs, Joseph J. "IN REAL LIFE: The Sane Multiculturalism of Brooklyn." *American Enterprise,* September 1, 1996, p. 73.

The Second Wave: Palestinian Immigrants: 1948–1967

2

Palestine, sometimes called the Holy Land, is a region about 175 miles long and 80 miles wide located roughly between the Jordan River and the east coast of the Mediterranean Sea. Jews and Arabs have lived in the region since their Hebrew and Philistine ancestors migrated there more than three thousand years ago. (The word "Palestine" is a Greek form of a Hebrew word meaning "land of the Philistines.")

During the first and second centuries, while the Roman Empire controlled Palestine, the Jews were severely persecuted (tyrannized), and most of them moved elsewhere. During the nineteenth and twentieth centuries, modern Jews faced terrible persecution in parts of Europe and Asia. Through an organized Zionist movement, they succeeded in convincing the United Nations (an international body established to promote world peace) to authorize the founding of the nation of Israel. The Palestinian region was to be divided into two countries: one a homeland for Jews and the other for Arabs. In 1948 nearly half of the Arabs living in Palestine were forced out of their homes; more than four hundred villages were crushed by bulldozers and rebuilt by the Israelis.

⊞ A Jewish Perspective

The state of Israel, carved out of Palestinian lands, has been the focus of war and controversy since it was created in 1948. The Palestinian Arabs believe their land was unjustly taken from them. Israelis, on the other hand, believe the land is rightfully theirs, promised to the Jewish people by God thousands of years ago. Cynthia Ozick, a Jewish American novelist, spoke at a 1998 conference called "The State of the Jewish State." Here is part of what she said:

> As for the cultural discomfort of minorities [Arabs in Israel] . . . if they are not harassed, if their religious institutions and schools are free to express what they wish, that is all that is required; the highest standard has been met. It is not the responsibility of governments to grant full and complete psychological comfort at all times and at every season to all its citizens (ask any American Jew at Christmastime). . . .
>
> [Israel] was not established in the negative, solely as a "haven" [safe place], though it gratefully serves that purpose too . . .; on the contrary, it was established as a national revolution toward Jewish freedom of self-expression—a freedom that can be found nowhere else in the world. Christianity and Islam have scores of countries offering Christian and Islamic self-expression; the Jewish people have only one country, still precarious [insecure], still under ferocious threat, still tender in years, still a sapling in need of nurture. (*Jerusalem Post,* December 25, 1998, p. 8.)

Twenty years later, Israel invaded additional Arab land and forced more Palestinians out of their homes.

At the end of the twentieth century, three-fourths of the world's 4.7 million Palestinian Arabs are recognized by the United Nations as being refugees from their homeland. (Refugees are people who leave their homes to escape war or political upheaval.) About 5,000 of them came directly to the United States; tens of thousands more came to America after living for a while in other countries. Because of such indirect migration, it is difficult to tell how many Palestinians entered the United States between 1948 and 1967, the "second wave" of Arab immigration. They and their children account for a Palestinian Arab American population that is estimated to be between 50,000 and 200,000. Most of them live in New York, New York, Chicago, Illinois, and parts of California and Virginia.

Many Palestinian Americans are working with Jewish Americans to improve understanding and cooperation between their peoples, a process that is easier to do in America than in the disputed territories of the Middle East. Various organizations around the United States sponsor events ranging from national conferences to local potluck dinners to encourage dialogue and friendship between Jews and Palestinians.

Encouraged by guarantees of freedom of speech in the United States, some Palestinian immigrants have publicly spoken or written their opinions about the progress of the Middle Eastern peace process. They hope to influence public opinion in this country, which may affect the government's policies. **Jamil I. Toubbeh** left Israel shortly after it was established; he has made the United States his home, but he is still deeply concerned about the future of Palestine. **Anton Shammas** came to America thirty years later; he still considers himself an exile and hopes someday to go back there. (An exile is a person who is forced to live outside his own country.) **Naomi Shihab Nye**, whose father fled Palestine, is an American and a Palestinian—through birth and through experience.

Jamil I. Toubbeh

Day of the Long Night:
A Palestinian Refugee Remembers the Nakba
Excerpt from the memoirs of Jamil I. Toubbeh
Published in 1998

The English word "holocaust," meaning a great devastation, is used as a name for the deliberate killing of six million European Jews by the Nazi government of Germany between 1933 and 1945. The Palestinian people use the Arabic word "nakba," meaning a catastrophe or disaster, to refer to their eviction from their homeland as a result of the founding of the Jewish nation of Israel in 1948. (Israel was created from Palestinian Arab lands.) According to Philip Mattar, executive director of the Institute for Palestine Studies, about one-half of the 780,000 Palestinians who left when Israel was created decided to go because they were afraid of violence, while the other half were forced to leave by the Israeli government. A second nakba happened after the 1967 Six Day War, when Israel captured Arab land that belonged to Jordan and Egypt; another 325,000 Palestinians left their homes.

The experience of Jamil I. Toubbeh (1930–) and his family is typical of what happened to Arab residents of Palestine. The Toubbehs left their home because of the frequent shootings, bombings, and knifings that were taking place in their neighborhood. They expected to return to their home

"Most Jews were surprised, and some were shocked, to learn that I, a Palestinian, had been driven out of my country by terror or by force at the hands of their own."

when the violence settled down, but they were never allowed back. Their house was torn down, and a new home was built there for Jewish settlers.

Like many Palestinians, Toubbeh emigrated to another country after he was driven from his home. He settled in the United States. His parents, like many other Palestinians who migrated to nearby Arab countries, settled in Jordan.

Things to remember while reading the excerpt from *Day of the Long Night: A Palestinian Refugee Remembers the Nakba:*

- Toubbeh grew up in Katamon, a section of Jerusalem located two miles outside the walls of the Old City.

- Palestine was ruled by Great Britain from 1918 until 1948. In the Balfour Declaration of 1917, the British government had promised the Jewish people a national home in Palestine.

- Both Arabs and Jews resorted to violence when land that belonged to Palestinians was given by the United Nations (an international organization established to promote world peace) to the new state of Israel. A barbed wire fence separated the city of Jerusalem into Israeli and Arab sectors.

Day of the Long Night: A Palestinian Refugee Remembers the Nakba

[In 1947, during the birth of Israel]

I was barely seventeen when my father finally decided to move the family away from one of Jerusalem's zones of terror. It was in November 1947. The steep hill overlooking our Katamon residence was a **haven** *for* **snipers**, *surely* **condoned** *by the European Jewish inhabitants of the . . . two massive, pink stone structures on top of the hill. The snipers could fire above the Swiss* **Consulate** *into the*

Haven: Safe place.

Snipers: People who shoot at other people from a hiding place.

Condoned: Accepted, allowed.

Consulate: Headquarters of an official representative of a foreign government.

heart of Katamon and beyond. Every morning, I would look through the black-and-gold lace curtain of our living-room window toward these buildings, hoping to see them in flames so that I could walk in peace to Terra Sancta College, my high school. The red-and-white Swiss flag above the consular building was always flying, always signaling hope. At the time, I did not know that our country and its people were being transformed into mythical beings by the fathers of **Zionism** and the protectors of our land, the British. I did not know that within months, the entire Palestinian population, except for a small minority of Jews, would become **personae non gratae.** Most shockingly, I did not know that we were about to be forced to **relinquish** many centuries of cultural **evolution,** our culture to be replaced by **alien** cultures of immigrants from the ghettos of Europe, the United States, the Soviet Union, and the rest of the world. . . .

As children, we invented and played games across the [barbed] wire, then learned to harass the British by triggering the harmless, explosive-smoke devices that alerted soldiers to **breaches** of security. **Yasser Arafat** and the rest of the Palestinian leadership were still in their mother's arms. It was fun watching the soldiers running up or down the slopes or bouncing in their trucks to replace the explosive devices long after we had escaped on both sides of the fence. We kept those young soldiers in good physical condition. . . .

[In 1951, emigrating to the United States]

I left Jerusalem in June 1951. Family and friends accompanied me to Kalandia Airport, a landing strip some miles north of Jerusalem. It was not an unusual morning in the mountains of Palestine: the sky was blue, the air chilly. My father and mother, obviously under strain, tried unsuccessfully to turn the **melancholy** occasion into a festive one. Their **muted utterances** mirrored their **doleful** mood. Someone was ordering family and friends to line up for pictures. "Don't forget," my father reminded me, "someone will be waiting for you at the airport in Beirut." It was small talk. He was concealing words of affection. I knew how he felt, and I hugged him in silence. We had said it all the night before. Then I hugged my mother, standing beside him. She was elegant, with a silk scarf around her powdered cheeks. Her reddish hair shivered in the morning breeze. She smiled as she looked into my eyes. "You have my brown and green eyes, my love."

"And you, **Im Michel,** have the most beautiful eyes in the world."

Zionism: A movement dedicated to the establishment and development of the state of Israel as a Jewish homeland.

Personae non gratae: People who are not welcome or acceptable.

Relinquish: Give up.

Evolution: Development.

Alien: Foreign.

Breaches: Breaks in.

Yasser Arafat: (also spelled Yasir; 1929–) head of the Palestine Liberation Organization (PLO) since 1968 and president of the Palestinian government-in-exile since 1996.

Melancholy: Sad.

Muted: Quiet.

Utterances: Words.

Doleful: Sad.

Im Michel: "Mother of Michael"; Palestinian adults are referred to as parents of their eldest son—or eldest daughter if they have no son.

*She did not have to remind me of her love. The mind has a way of scanning millions of experiences in seconds, freezing priceless moments to prove the **inviolability** of parental love. She held back her tears as I turned to hug each family member and friend. My two nephews—Hani, nine years old, and Riyad, six—waited in the distance with their father. Both would later work with the **Palestine Liberation Organization**, and Hani would die in 1976, at age thirty-seven, filming the war in Lebanon's mountains. I hugged them and promised to return soon.*

The pilot of the twin-engine plane waited patiently while family and friends exchanged words of hope about my departure and safe arrival. I climbed the plane's short ladder, and in moments, we were airborne. Aloft, the plane veered quickly to the north, then east, avoiding Jewish state boundaries. At five hundred feet, I could see the scattered crowd waving goodbye. I returned the gesture, though I knew no one would see it. The sight of my parents wiping tears from their eyes was a farewell I can never forget. Perhaps they sensed that I would not see them for a very long time. . . .

*Customs and immigration officials were cordial. Sean [an American friend] sped through formalities while I waited for officials to search my bags, fingerprint me, and ask me to "repeat after" them, under oath, that I was not a **communist**, had never been one, had not belonged or ever belonged to a communist organization. I did not then understand these concerns and had not yet heard of **Joseph R. McCarthy**. I signed where I was told to sign, wondering about America's obsession with "isms." Moments later, I was directed to the passport checkpoint, where I was greeted by a middle-aged woman who asked me to consider changing my name to a more suitable American name. "James Tobias would be a very good name for you because it sounds like your name and people won't have problems pronouncing it," she advised. . . .*

[In 1967 in the United States, just after the Six Day War]

*Most Jews were surprised, and some were shocked, to learn that I, a Palestinian, had been driven out of my country by terror or by force at the hands of their own. My presence and my **demeanor** were a contradiction to all they had learned concerning Palestine and Palestinians. When he was a young Zionist volunteer, [an acquaintance of mine] had not been informed that Katamon, Jerusalem or the Jewish state was **occupied** territory, nor had he been made aware that he was a silent partner in its **conveyance** to European, Russian, and American Jews. He could not **fathom** that*

Inviolability: Indestructibility.

Palestine Liberation Organization (PLO): A political and military group that represents the Palestinian people in negotiations with Israel; it is considered in the Arab world the Palestinian government-in-exile.

Communist: A supporter of a form of government that allows little private ownership of property.

Joseph R. McCarthy: (1908–1957) U.S. senator who led a national anticommunist movement during the 1950s.

Demeanor: Appearance.

Occupied: Governed by another country under forced rule.

Conveyance: Transfer.

Fathom: Understand.

*my family had owned property in Palestine. No Jew would admit that his or her own people could be so cruel as to **dispossess** another of its property, roots, or culture. This would be **anathema** to the Jews' self-professed **humanitarianism**. In the 1980s and 1990s, the Jewish religious right shattered this psychological barrier as it evicted Palestinians from their homes **relentlessly** and **remorselessly**. . . .*

The question arises as to whether there is hope for a just and peaceful resolution of the Palestinian dilemma. The answer is "yes"; the formula is simple. Allow Palestinians to return to and resettle their ancestral land, country that was Palestinian Arab only fifty years ago and, prior to that time, for generations. Then, declare January 1, 2000, "Independence Day" for a new state whose boundaries would be those of 1948. (Toubbeh, Day of the Long Night, *pp. 9, 13–15, 103, 105, 119, 157)*

What happened next . . .

By trying to inform citizens and government officials about what really happened to the Palestinian Arabs, Toubbeh hopes to change American policy that he believes has supported the nakba. He sees clear parallels between the experiences of the Palestinians and the Native American people—both groups lost their homes to invaders who claimed the land as their own. In addition to the return of the lands of Israel into Palestinian hands, he would like to see a change in U.S. national policy that would help Native Americans rebuild their ancestral communities.

Did you know . . .

- In 1903 the British government offered the Jews land in Uganda, Africa, where they could establish their national home. They declined, hoping to reestablish their nation in the area surrounding Jerusalem, a region from which they had been driven out by the conquering Romans in the second century.

Dispossess: Take from; steal.

Anathema: Something that is hated or condemned.

Humanitarianism: Love of mankind.

Relentlessly: Without yielding; firmly.

Remorselessly: Without guilt.

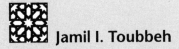

Jamil I. Toubbeh

Born in 1930, Jamil I. Toubbeh was one of ten children of the *mukhtar* (respected leader) of the Katamon district of Jerusalem, Palestine (now Israel). When he was seventeen, Toubbeh and his family left their home in search of safety from escalating violence between Jews and Arabs. After staying for a while in the apartment of a married older sister, they moved into a house belonging to a wealthy family that was staying in its vacation home outside violent Jerusalem. Finally, Toubbeh and his family moved into a Greek Orthodox (Christian) convent, along with many other refugees.

In 1951, his parents sent Toubbeh to the United States to escape the turmoil of his homeland and attend college. He earned a Ph.D. (Doctorate) in psychology from the University of Illinois. After working for ten years for the U.S. Department of Health, Education, and Welfare (now Health and Human Services), Toubbeh began working for the U.S. Indian Health Service in 1976. For more than twenty years, he has continued to work with Native Americans, especially those with physical or mental disabilities.

- Zionism began in the nineteenth century, when Jews were being persecuted in Russia and Austria. At first, it was an unorganized migration of individual families from a hostile environment to the land of their ancient ancestors. Following the 1897 World Zionist Congress, organizations were formed all over the world to work toward the establishment of a Jewish nation in Palestine.

- With both Arabs and Jews claiming the right to Palestine as a homeland, violence erupted long before the United Nations authorized the formation of Israel in 1947. There were three significant riots during the 1920s and an Arab rebellion that lasted from 1936 to 1939.

For More Information

Ameri, Anan, and Dawn Ramey, eds. *Arab American Encyclopedia.* Farmington Hills, MI: U•X•L, 2000.

Mattar, Philip. "Palestine." *Microsoft Encarta 96 Encyclopedia.* Funk & Wagnalls, 1995.

Toubbeh, Jamil I. *Day of the Long Night: A Palestinian Refugee Remembers the Nakba.* Jefferson, NC: McFarland, 1998.

Anton Shammas

"Palestinians in Israel: You Ain't Seen Nothin' Yet"

Selection from a speech
Delivered in April 1995
Published in the Fall 1995 issue of
ii: The Journal of the International Institute

Israel was established by authority of the United Nations, a world body dedicated to keeping peace among countries, as a homeland for Jewish people in 1948. Since the late nineteenth century, numerous people worked tirelessly for the cause of Zionism, a movement dedicated to establishing a Jewish state in the Middle East. After the Holocaust of World War II (1939–45), in which more than six million Jews were murdered by German leader Adolf Hitler and his Nazi Party, the plight of the Jews gained immediacy. The United Nations determined that Palestine was to be divided into two countries: one a homeland for Jews and the other for Arabs. War immediately erupted between the two groups. When the war was over and Israel emerged victorious, 780,000 Palestinians were forced to leave their homes in the area that became Israel. However, 156,000 Palestinian residents of the area stayed there. Through later wars, Israel took more land from neighboring countries, increasing the number of Palestinians living within its borders. Though these Arabs and their children are citizens of Israel, their rights and protections are less than those of Jewish citizens.

"Why is it that whenever there is an attempt to illuminate the Mideastern conflicts, the Israeli point of view is always heard first . . . so the Palestinian point of view is forever given as a response, losing a great deal of validity, urgency and relevance right on the outset?"

حلويات الشرق

Youths wave the Israeli-banned Palestinian flag as they hurl stones and charge towards Israeli soldiers during demonstrations in Nablus, in the West Bank, December 12, 1987. Though some Arabs are citizens of Israel, their rights and protections are less than those of Jewish citizens.
Reproduced by permission of Reuters/Corbis–Bettmann.

Although he is not Jewish, Anton Shammas (1950–) wants to be a full citizen of Israel because he was born and raised there. In the 1980s in Israel he worked as a journalist, writing for newspapers and magazines and television. When he began publishing articles about what he considered unfair treatment of the Arab citizens of Israel, he became unpopular with some violent groups of Israeli Jews. After being threatened by terrorists, he fled to the United States in 1987. He hopes it will someday be safe for him to return to Israel; in the meantime, he lives in Michigan with his wife (an Israeli Jew) and his two children (who are American citizens because they were born in America).

Things to remember while reading "Palestinians in Israel: You Ain't Seen Nothin' Yet":

- Most countries consider citizenship and nationality the same thing; for example, a citizen of America is American and a citizen of France is French. However, the government of Israel does not recognize "Israeli" as a nationality. On each citizen's identity card, that government classifies him or her as a Jew, an Arab, or a Druze (a member of a particular Islamic sect).

- Shammas thinks that because the Israeli point of view has been more prominently presented in the media, most people believe it is right and that the Palestinian Arab point of view, therefore, must be wrong.

- Shammas believes that a country called Palestine should be established and that the state of Israel should continue to exist. But he also believes that Palestinian citizens of Israel should be able to stay in Israel and enjoy the rights and benefits of full citizenship.

"Palestinians in Israel: You Ain't Seen Nothin' Yet"

*In my own journalistic writings since the early 80s, especially in the **Hebrew** press, I have been examining what I think of—and I might be dead wrong—as the best of possible **discourses** on the matter [of the Palestinian citizens of Israel]. I have been examining, from within and from without, the limits and the **elasticity** of that very controversial term, "Israeli nationality." I think that . . . there's only one way out for the Palestinians of Israel, a way out from the ethno-political **ghetto** they have been squeezed into since 1948: to challenge from within the very definition of the state of Israel as a Jewish state which is an ethnic **democracy** that presents itself to the outside world in an **ingenious PR hoax**, as a nation state and "the only democracy in the Middle East." In other, more blunt words, this would mean to un-Jew the state of Israel, to de-Judaicize it, and make it the state of its citizens, instead of "the state of the Jewish people," as it defines itself. . . .*

*This means that once the Israeli–Palestinian question is settled, via the two-state solution (which I **ardently** support), and once there is a Palestinian state beside Israel, on the morning after—the hard core of the Israeli–Palestinian conflict will not have been solved yet.*

Hebrew: The traditional language of the Jews.

Discourses: Discussions.

Elasticity: Flexibility; bendability.

Ghetto: Confined, inferior space.

Democracy: A form of government in which leaders are elected by the people and in which all people stand equal before the law.

Ingenious: Brilliant.

PR: Public relations.

Hoax: Lie.

Ardently: Strongly.

And that hard core . . . is: What's to be done with the 800,000 Palestinian citizens of Israel, whose problem was kept on hold for five decades? Hence the ticking quality of the "you ain't seen nothin' yet" in my subtitle. . . .

I've been living in [the United States] for the last eight years or so, perhaps the most fateful years in the recent history of the Middle East. And since the day I arrived, I keep wondering why is it that everywhere you turn the Israeli discourse is always the **privileged** one, the one that has the upper hand; why is it that whenever there is an attempt to **illuminate** the Mideastern conflicts, the Israeli point of view is always heard first, asserting itself as a **point of discursive departure**, and as the only **point of reference**, so the Palestinian point of view is forever given as a response, losing a great deal of **validity**, urgency and **relevance** right on the outset?. . .

What I'm trying to raise is an issue that reflects, ever so precisely, the prevalent Western attitudes toward the Middle East. Nations who have a state, can have a claim to a language, a voice, a discourse. They can effectively impose their point of view and make it the **most audible** one around; and the most audible point of view, we the media-products know, is the right point of view. On the other hand, stateless nations cannot have a claim to a language, but have to make do with a **dialect**, that has no voice, has no discourse. . . .

I have been using the term "the Palestinians of Israel" quite matter-of-factly throughout these remarks. The truth is that to this very day there are still Jewish Israelis who believe that the mere introduction of the word Palestine in order to refer to an "internal Israeli problem," so to speak, is highly **subversive**. The truth is that there are still "Israeli Arabs," to use the official terminology, who are very reluctant and afraid to define themselves as Palestinians. This goes back, of course, to the days when the Palestinians, as a people, did not even exist, as the late **Golda Meir** informed us at the time.

It was not before the beginning of the 70s that "the Arabs of Israel" began, almost **illicitly**, to refer to themselves, in one way or another, as Israeli citizens who belong to the Palestinian people. To the best of my knowledge, the first Israeli official, and a high ranking one at that, to define them as Palestinians was Mosheh Arens [1925–], the then-chairman of the Security and Foreign Affairs Committee [in 1981]. . . .

Privileged: Favored.

Illuminate: Shed light on.

Point of discursive departure: Beginning point of a discussion.

Point of reference: A standard belief; a view whose truth is taken for granted.

Validity: Being thought of as true and justified.

Relevance: Importance.

Most audible: Easiest to hear; loudest.

Dialect: A variation of a language.

Subversive: Rebellious; disloyal.

Golda Meir: (1898–1978) Israeli prime minister from 1969 until 1974.

Illicitly: Not legally permitted.

Naming, as you know, is a powerful thing, a privilege given to those who have the power. And what Arens seemed to have **inadvertently** done, was to admit, on the highest official level, that the "Arabs of Israel" are, in effect, a part of the "Palestinian Problem," or the "Palestinian Question," and that every future settlement of the Palestinian–Israeli conflict should take this fact into full consideration. But judging from the **Oslo agreement** it seems that everybody was wrong: the "Arabs of Israel" are not a part of any solution; on the contrary, the absence of any reference to them in all the political negotiations that have been going on in recent years, between Israel and the **PLO**, shows that they are, still, a part of the problem, and not the solution.

The Palestinians of Israel are a part of the problem because their problem will not be solved by the establishment of a Palestinian state. If anything, the establishment of that state, I believe, will create the false belief that their national **grievances** have been dealt with and that their complaints about inequality on all levels have been addressed. Unless, of course, they opt for the **intifada** way. . . .

A decade ago or so, a group of scholars in the School of Law at Tel-Aviv University, came up with a proposal for a constitution for the state of Israel. . . . As you know, Israel does not have a constitution. . . . But bear in mind that the Israeli Declaration of Independence promised a constitution no later than October first, 1948. Many Octobers, since that one, have elapsed.

The first sentence in the Tel-Aviv proposal states that "The State of Israel is the state of the Jewish people" (the Hebrew original, unlike the authorized English translation of the proposal, adds: "for eternity," to be on the safe side). Then the drafters go on, ten lines down, to declare that "The State of Israel is a democratic state." Which is exactly what the Declaration of Independence had done in 1948; which means that we are back to square one: no state can be a democratic state if it is not the state of its citizens. Incidentally, that is exactly the same grave mistake that the Palestinians made in their own Declaration of Independence, in 1988: "The State of Palestine is the state of Palestinians wherever they are," the Palestinian Declaration stated; and this was not the only **lethal plagiarism** in that text. As time goes by, it's very evident that the Palestinians are going to **emulate** all the mistakes of **Zionism**: ethnic state, **Law of Return**, and all the rest of it. (Shammas, "Palestinians")

Inadvertently: Mistakenly; without thinking.

Oslo agreement: A 1993 peace agreement between the Palestinians and Israelis that called for Israeli withdrawal from certain Palestinian regions.

PLO: Palestine Liberation Organization; a political and military group that represents the Palestinian people in negotiations with Israel; it is considered in the Arab world the Palestinian government-in-exile.

Grievances: Complaints.

Intifada: A civilian resistance movement by Palestinians against the Israeli government.

Lethal: Deadly.

Plagiarism: Copying someone else's words.

Emulate: Imitate.

Zionism: A movement dedicated to the establishment of the state of Israel as a Jewish homeland.

Law of Return: A law of Israel that allows a Jew from any country to move to Israel and immediately become a full citizen.

The Second Wave: Palestinian Immigrants: Anton Shammas

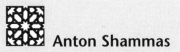

Anton Shammas

In 1950 Anton Shammas was born in the village of Fassuta in northern Israel, a nation that had existed for only two years. Twelve years later, he moved to the larger city of Haifa along with his parents and his five older brothers. Because he was a Christian Arab, he was treated like an outsider by the Jewish Israelis of Haifa. After six unhappy years in that city, Shammas moved to Jerusalem to attend college.

Arabic was Shammas's native language, but after he moved to Haifa he decided he must learn Hebrew, the traditional Jewish language. He worked very hard until he could speak and write Hebrew as though it had been his first language. Basing it on his own life, he wrote a novel called *Arabesques* so Israeli Jews would understand what it was like to be an Israeli Arab. He wrote the book in Hebrew so it would be understandable and meaningful for Jewish readers. It quickly became a best-seller when it was published in 1986.

In addition to his novel, Shammas wrote political essays in newspapers and

Anton Shammas. *Reproduced by permission of Jerry Bauer.*

magazines expressing his view that Israel should not be a Jewish state, but a nation in which all citizens had equal rights regardless of their race or religion. These views upset a Jewish terrorist group, which painted graffiti on his apartment building and telephoned him with death threats. In 1987 he fled in fear and moved to Michigan.

What happened next . . .

Because they signed the Oslo Agreement in 1993, Palestinian leader Yasir Arafat (1929–) and Israeli Prime Minister Yitzhak Rabin (1922–1995) were awarded the Nobel Peace Prize. However, the hoped-for peaceful solution to the Palestinian problem has not yet happened. The Israelis and the Palestinians accuse each other of not living up to the terms of the Oslo Agreement. In 1998 leaders of the two groups met again and signed the Wye River Memorandum, which detailed a time frame for specific steps each side would take toward a peaceful solution. Because neither side trusted the other, the steps were not accomplished on schedule. With a change in Israeli leadership in 1999, however, hopes for peace talks—and consequent peace—were renewed.

Did you know . . .

- Besides having published numerous essays and a novel, Shammas also writes poetry. In 1997 he wrote an Arabic-language play called *Wash your Face O Moon,* about the loss of traditional identity by Palestinian Israelis.

- Shammas's novel *Arabesques* has been published in seven languages. The *New York Times* named it one of the seven best works of fiction in 1988, when the English translation was published.

- Eighty-one percent of the population of Israel is Jewish. Of the non-Jewish population, 75 percent are Muslim Arabs, 16 percent are Christian Arabs, and about 9 percent are Druze.

For More Information

Hall, Loretta, and Bridget K. Hall. "Anton Shammas." *Arab American Biography.* Farmington Hills, MI: U•X•L, 1999.

Shammas, Anton. "Palestinians in Israel: You Ain't Seen Nothin' Yet." *ii: The Journal of the International Institute* (Fall 1995). Available at http://www.umich.edu/~iinet/journal/vol3no1/palest.html (March 1999).

Naomi Shihab Nye

"Banned Poem"

**Selection from an essay written in 1992
Published in 1994 in *Food for Our Grandmothers*,
edited by Joanna Kadi**

The Intifada was a civilian (nonmilitary) uprising by Palestinian Arabs living under Israeli rule. It involved activities such as refusing to pay taxes or to buy Israeli products, marching in peaceful demonstrations, throwing rocks at Israeli soldiers, and occasionally hurling firebombs at Israeli tanks. The Intifada (pronounced in-tay-FAH-dah) began in December 1987 and lasted more than five years. It gave Palestinians a sense of pride in their resistance to military conquest. Palestinian emigrants participated by sending money, food, and medical supplies to the protestors.

The Israelis responded harshly. For example, they imposed curfews, forbidding people to be out in public places at certain times; they denied permission for many Palestinians to go from one city (where they lived) to another (where they worked); and they attacked Palestinian homes with tear gas and gunfire. Hundreds of people, both Palestinian and Israeli, were killed. Because the Intifada activities, many of which were peaceful protests, were conducted by civilians rather than by armies, they helped arouse international public opinion in sympathy for the Palestinians. They helped soften the

"In my mind a censor is a huge hulking man at a wide desk with a cigar and a massive inkpad for stamping NO NO NO. . . . I say how often journalism has frustrated me, and maybe that is why the world needs poetry, too."

A Palestinian youth hurls a stone from a large sling towards Israeli soldiers in the Anata refugee camp outside Jerusalem, January 1988. The Intifada gave Palestinians a sense of pride in their resistance to military conquest. *Reproduced by permission of Corbis/Reuters.*

image of Palestinian leader Yasir Arafat (1929–), who had developed a reputation as a terrorist as the longtime leader of the Palestine Liberation Organization (PLO), the most prominent of the political and military groups who fought the Israeli government.

In 1992, Naomi Shihab Nye (1952–), an American poet whose father was a Palestinian immigrant, visited her ancestral home in the West Bank of the Jordan River, a region that Israel took from Jordan in 1967. Nye, who also writes essays, recorded her observations and experiences in several articles, including one called "Banned Poem."

Things to remember while reading the selection from "Banned Poem":

- In some countries, the government can control what is published in newspapers and magazines. This is called censorship; government agents who read material submitted for publication are called censors. If they think the material is objectionable (usually because it criticizes the government), they can delete portions of it or block its publication entirely.

- Nye's father came to the United States at the age of eighteen. When Nye was fourteen, she and her family lived in Jordan for a year while her father worked as editor of the *Jerusalem Times* newspaper. Other than for that year, Nye lived in Missouri and Texas while she was growing up.

"Banned Poem"
(East Jerusalem 1992)

*The Palestinian **journalists** have gathered in a small, modestly elegant theater that could have dropped out of any neighborhood in Paris or New York. We are shivering, having just whirled through a gust of bone-chilling wind on the street outside. Our friend tells us it is always cold and windy on this one street.*

*Mulling together with their notebooks, the journalists—mostly men in dark jackets, a few using **kaffiyehs** for scarves—speak quietly. Some sit at tables, smoking over small cups of coffee and plates of sweets.*

*I feel overcome by a speaker's worst horror—nothing to say. Too much, and nothing. What could I possibly say that these people might want to hear? Why would a group of **beleaguered** journalists wish to listen to a Palestinian-American poet who lives in Texas?*

We shake hands, greet, get introduced. The niceties of human encounter weigh heavily upon the room. . . .

Because it is not hard to have some idea of their situation, and because their faces house such strong dignity nonetheless, I keep asking questions. How do you stand this life here? How do you sustain hope?

And the answers come slowly, cloaked in the mystery which says, "We keep on going. See? We wake up and we keep on going."

Journalists: News reporters.

Kaffiyeh: (kuh-FEE-yuh) An Arab headdress consisting of a cloth draped over the head that is held in place by a cord encircling the head.

Beleaguered: Besieged; overburdened.

Amidst daily curfews, closures, and beatings, my friend the bookseller arranges her lovely series of British Ladybird books for children. "I never know, on any given day, if I will be able to come to work, since I live in the next town." . . .

*My new friend the English professor teaches contemporary American and British literatures behind a university door riddled with at least fifty **ungrammatical** bullet holes. Israeli soldiers approached the campus recently while the students held a small party, a rare occurrence in Intifada times, to celebrate the end of semester. "The party had nothing to do with politics," he tells me. "You know that relief which comes after exams, before break, that sense of lightened load and sweeter days? A very momentary sense, I can assure you, particularly here in the **Occupied Territories**. My students were eating cake when the soldiers started shouting outside. The students called down to them, 'This is a private gathering,' and they started shooting. Believe me, there was no more **provocation** than that. We are leaving the door with the bullet holes to remind us of the terrible times we live in."*

*The times. They are hard to forget. And the journalists carry notebooks and pens, though every paragraph they write must first be submitted to the Israeli censors. In my mind a **censor** is a huge hulking man at a wide desk with a cigar and a massive inkpad for stamping NO NO NO. The journalists file into their seats. I say how often journalism has frustrated me, and maybe that is why the world needs poetry, too.*

After the start of the Intifada, our local newspaper in Texas ticked off the Palestinian dead in tiny token back-page notes: seventy-sixth Palestinian dead, 425th Palestinian dead—as if keeping score in a sporting event. Only when the number fattened to a ripe 500 did the victim receive a story. Ibtisam Bozieh, age thirteen. She'd dreamed of becoming a doctor, but was shot in the face by an Israeli soldier when she peered curiously through the window of her village home, perhaps to see what was going on out there.

After reading that slim story, I could not stop thinking about Ibtisam Bozieh. She followed me, in waking, in troubled sleep. A small poem was born, written to her, which includes the lines, "When do we become doctors for one another, Arab, Jew, instead of guarding tumors of pain as if they hold us upright?"

The journalists ask for a copy of the poem. I read a few others. I try to tell them, in a way they may believe, how many Americans I

Ungrammatical: Defying the laws of language.

Occupied Territories: Formerly Palestinian land controlled by the Israeli government through its armed forces.

Provocation: Something that causes an action or event.

Censor: A government agent charged with blocking the publication of pieces of text or whole texts they deem objectionable.

know, both writers and otherwise, who have their interests at heart. But quite obviously we do not run the government. They grow energetic. They tell me we will meet tomorrow too, same theater, same hour. . . .

*Next day a small **hubbub** greets us in the theater, brimming with excitement. . . .*

Yesterday after our meeting the journalists translated my poem about Ibtisam into Arabic on the spot. I can picture them—smoking, arguing over words. They submitted it to the censors with the rest of their stories last night. It came back today slashed with red X's, stamped at the bottom of the page, REJECTED ENTIRELY, in Arabic and Hebrew. The journalists have encircled it with barbed wire and placed it on red velvet under a frame, presenting it to me at the microphone in front of the crowd, a gift to take home. So I may remember them and the shape of their days. "Now you are one of us," they say. It's a strangely honorable linkage, to be rejected by their own censors.

Think of it: two peoples, so closely related it's hard to tell them apart in the streets sometimes, claiming the same land. The end of the twentieth century.

*I keep shuddering. I keep feeling gripped, as if someone has placed an icy hand on my shoulder. None of this does any good for Ibtisam, of course. She's probably buried in her high-up village between the craggy, endlessly patient olive trees. It seems wrong to me that soldiers wear olive-colored **fatigues**. (Nye in Kadi, pp. 97–100)*

What happened next . . .

In 1993, a year after Nye wrote "Banned Poem," international pressure prevailed on the leaders of Israel and the Palestinian people. They signed the Oslo Agreement, in which Israel officially recognized the existence of a Palestinian government and agreed to withdraw from the West Bank of the Jordan River and the Gaza Strip on the Mediterranean coast.

Hubbub: Uproar.

Fatigues: Military clothing worn for combat duty.

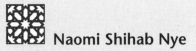

Naomi Shihab Nye

Born in 1952, Nye grew up in St. Louis, Missouri. Her father was a Palestinian Arab, and her mother was of Swiss and German ancestry. In 1966 the family moved to the West Bank, which was part of Jordan, so Nye, her brother, and her mother could learn about her father's culture. She attended school in Jerusalem, a city that had been divided since Israel was created in 1948. From her classroom window she could see barbed wire fences that separated the Israeli and Jordanian parts of the city. In 1967 Israel, believing it was about to be invaded by Egypt, attacked Egypt and Jordan. Nye and her family managed to return to the United States just days before the fighting began. The Six Day War was over quickly; when it ended, Israel had taken control of several pieces of territory including the Gaza Strip, an area on the Mediterranean coast, and the West Bank of the Jordan River.

After graduating from college, Nye conducted creative writing workshops in schools in addition to writing poetry and

Naomi Shihab Nye. *Reproduced by permission of Bill Kennedy.*

essays. Believing that it is important for people of different cultures to understand each other, she has edited several multicultural books of poetry. She married Michael Nye, a photographer, in 1978. They live in San Antonio, Texas, with their son.

Did you know . . .

- Nye's trip to Jerusalem in 1992 was one of three speaking tours she made to the Middle East and Asia under the sponsorship of the United States Information Agency (USIA). The purpose of such tours is to build understanding between Americans and citizens of other nations.

- Nye is also an anthologist: she has published several collections of poetry written by people from many countries. *The Space between Our Footsteps,* published in 1998, contains works by poets from twenty Middle Eastern nations, including both Israel and Palestine. "When I used poetry from Israeli and Palestinian women, it showed how poetically the women were aligned," she told a reporter for the *St. Louis Post–Dispatch.* "One Palestinian mother had lost a son in the fighting, and so had an Israeli mother."

For More Information

Hall, Loretta, and Bridget K. Hall. "Naomi Shihab Nye." *Arab American Biography.* Farmington Hills, MI: U•X•L, 1999.

Hudson, Repps. "Anthologist Builds Bridges of Words across Middle Eastern Chasms." *St. Louis Post–Dispatch,* June 18, 1998, p. G1.

Nye, Naomi Shihab. "Banned Poem." *Food for Our Grandmothers: Writings by Arab-American and Arab-Canadian Feminists,* edited by Joanna Kadi. Boston: South End Press, 1994.

Schneider, Bart, ed. *Race, an Anthology in the First Person.* New York: Three Rivers Press, 1997.

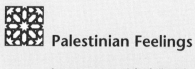

Palestinian Feelings

In an essay titled "Widening the Circle," Naomi Shihab Nye reveals her feelings as a Palestinian:

> Like thousands of others, my Palestinian relatives had lost their home and money in the bank to Zionists when the state of Israel was formed in 1948. [Zionists are dedicated to the establishment and development of the state of Israel as a Jewish homeland.] They gazed longingly across the no-man's-land toward the old stone house they could no longer see. . . . The Palestinians were, to the Jews, what the black population was to white St. Louis—second-class citizens, unfortunate realities, undeserving "others." . . .

> Each time I returned to the West Bank as an adult, I had experiences that made me grit my teeth and swear—guns pointed in my face, rough interrogations [questioning], witnessing vicious attacks of Arab citizens, tear gas, and despicable [hateful] rudeness on the part of those with weapons. . . .

> Luckily, I met many Jews over the years, both in the United States and Israel, who had a deeper concept of what the Jewish-Arab relationship could and should have been—cousins, from the start. (Nye in Schneider, pp. 38–40)

The Third Wave: Arab Immigration from Other Lands: 1967 to the Present

In response to the large number of immigrants who wanted to enter the United States after World War II (1939–45), the U.S. government enacted the Immigration and Nationality Act of 1952. The act established new quotas, or limits, that specified how many persons could immigrate from certain countries, although it allowed additional immigration by refugees and close relatives of people who had already immigrated. (Refugees are people who leave their homes to escape war or political upheaval.) In 1965 a new immigration law was enacted, doing away with the quota system. Within three years, the annual number of Arab immigrants jumped from 3,900 in 1965 to 7,200 in 1968. Arab immigration continued to increase; by 1992 the number was 27,000.

During this "third wave" of Arab immigration, people from Lebanon formed the largest group, about 20 percent. Palestinians who were removed from their homes when the state of Israel was created from Palestinian lands in 1948, and who fled the region on account of consequent Arab–Israeli wars, formed a substantial group. The number of Palestinian immigrants is unknown, however, because immigration

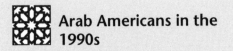

Arab Americans in the 1990s

In 1990 the population of the United States included approximately one million Arab Americans. According to U.S. census data, 63 percent were born in the United States (as descendants of immigrants). Of the foreign-born Arabs living in the United States in 1990, more than 75 percent arrived as part of the third wave of Arab immigration.

While the first and second waves consisted primarily of Christian Arabs, the third wave has been mostly Muslim. By 1991, approximately one-half of the Arab American population was Christian, and half was Muslim.

The 1990 U.S. census found that 60 percent of all Americans over the age of sixteen were employed, but among Arab Americans the figure was 80 percent. Compared to Americans as a whole, a larger proportion of Arab Americans has attended college; the percentage of Arab Americans with graduate degrees is twice as high as the national average.

Ten metropolitan areas in the United States are home to 36 percent of all Arab Americans. In all but two of those metropolitan areas, the income of Arab Americans is higher than the average of the general population.

records do not identify Palestinians who lived in another country, such as Jordan, before coming to the United States. Egypt and Jordan each account for about 17 percent of the Arab immigrants. Syrians made up 11 percent, and Iraqis about 9 percent. Immigration from Yemen increased at the fastest rate, quadrupling from 485 in 1982 to 2,100 in 1992.

The series of civil and international wars in the Middle East contributed to the third wave of immigration. **Mojahid Daoud**'s family, for example, left Jordan after Palestinian refugees from Israel poured into the country, draining its economic resources. After a violent revolution established a new government in **Shameem Rassam Amal**'s home country of Iraq in 1979, the country fought a war with Iran that lasted eight years. Two years after that war ended, Iraq invaded Kuwait, sparking the short but terribly destructive Gulf War of 1991.

Since the late 1800s, men from Yemen have supported their families by working in other countries where jobs were more available. Some, like **Anisa**'s husband, came to the United States, while others worked in Arab countries closer to home. Because of the Gulf War, 1.5 million Yemenis were forced to look for jobs—and homes—farther from their native country.

Anisa

"Anisa"

**Selection from *Family and Gender among American Muslims*,
edited by Barbara C. Aswad and Barbara Bilgé
Published in 1996**

Yemen, a country located on the southwestern part of the Arabian Peninsula, is about twice the size of the state of Wyoming. Because of its location at the base of the Red Sea, Yemen became important when construction of the Suez Canal (completed in 1869) allowed ships to sail between England and India by way of the Red and Mediterranean Seas without going all the way around Africa. To ensure the free passage of its ships along this route, Great Britain took control of the southern part of the region in the mid-1800s. British rule continued until 1967, when South Yemen (officially the People's Democratic Republic of Yemen) gained its independence. North Yemen was governed by local tribal leaders until 1962, when the Yemen Arab Republic was established.

In the 1980s, these two countries were among the least economically developed countries of the world. Because they produced little—there is only a small amount of arable land—they depended on financial aid from foreign countries. Another key to the survival of their people was money sent home by men who worked in other countries: in the early 1980s, more than one million Yemeni men supported their

"At first, I was excited about doing something new and different, but when I got here it was so difficult for me. I was so lonely. There was no one for me to talk to, nowhere for me to go. That was the worst part, being so lonely."

A group of Arab Americans crossing the street outside of the Yemen Cafe in Brooklyn, New York, March 1993. During her interview, Anisa wore a customary shapeless, ankle-length black dress, but the scarf on her head was pushed back so some of her hair showed, contrary to Muslim custom. Her teenage daughters were dressed in jeans, and their hair was completely uncovered. *Reproduced by permission of AP/Wide World Photos.*

families in this way. A moderate amount of oil was discovered in North Yemen in the 1980s, and development of this resource improved economic conditions there. In 1990, with financial support dwindling because of the collapse of the Union of Soviet Socialist Republics (USSR), South Yemen joined with North Yemen to form the Republic of Yemen.

There are two types of Yemeni people living in the United States. One group, the settlers, consists of true immigrants who intend to stay in America. The second group does not intend to stay. According to the October 1997 issue of the *Yemen Times,* "about 75% of the Yemenis [in America in the 1990s] are non-settlers, the so-called sojourners who live a cyclic life of movement. They go to the [United States] to work for several years and return to Yemen to spend several months with their families. Then they repeat the same cycle."

About 1990, Linda Walbridge, an anthropologist (a scientist who studies the development of cultures), interviewed several Arab immigrants who lived in Michigan. To encourage them to talk openly about their experiences and thoughts, Walbridge changed their names when she wrote descriptions of the interviews in *Family and Gender among American Muslims*. "Anisa," one of the people she interviewed, was a Yemeni woman who came to the United States with her husband in the 1970s.

Things to remember while reading "Anisa":

- Anisa is a Muslim, but not a very strict one. During Walbridge's interview, Anisa wore a customary shapeless, ankle-length black dress. Contrary to tradition, however, the scarf on her head was pushed back so some of her hair showed. Her teenage daughters were dressed in jeans, and their hair was completely uncovered.

- Anisa follows the Muslim practice of praying five times a day, and she and her husband fast (that is, they do not eat between sunrise and sunset) during Ramadan, the month of repentance (praying for forgiveness). She helps teach English to Arabic-speaking women at her mosque (place of worship).

- Anisa is happy that today some families in Yemen allow their daughters to go out with boys. She thinks it is good for a girl to get to know a man before she marries him.

"Anisa"

It is so different for them [my two teenage daughters] growing up than it was for me. When they don't have school, they sleep until 11:00 A.M. and then sit and watch TV. When I was young I got up at six or six thirty and prepared breakfast. I was the only daughter, so I had to do all the work. When I was small I played outside with my friends. We played hopscotch, blind man's bluff, games like that. But when a girl becomes eleven or twelve she is not allowed to play anymore. Then, I stayed inside and watched TV which was only on in the evenings, not like here. . . .

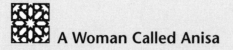

A Woman Called Anisa

Anisa grew up in Aden, one of the world's busiest seaports, in southern Yemen. Until she was thirteen years old, her father lived in the United States, where he operated a restaurant. Anisa, her two brothers, and her mother lived with her uncle until her father moved back to Yemen.

Anisa never dated boys. She married a distant cousin when she was eighteen; he had been working in America, and he wrote to her father asking if he could marry Anisa. She remembered him from when they were children, and she agreed to marry him. After their wedding, Anisa and her husband stayed for a month in her parents' home, and then they moved to Dearborn, Michigan, where many Yemeni immigrants live.

Anisa and her husband had two sons and two daughters. After nineteen years in America, Anisa and her husband still consider themselves Yemenis, and they want their children to keep their ethnic identity. Participating in social activities organized by the Yemeni community in Dearborn helps the family nurture that identity.

Only about 3 percent of parents allowed their daughters to go to high school. . . . I went because my mother wanted me to, because she had never had a chance. . . .

My boys used to help me around the house. . . . They would clean floors, wash the dishes, everything. Now they say that that work is just for girls. . . . Both my sons want to become doctors. . . .

Some Yemeni husbands don't want their wives to work. They don't want them to go out. My husband is not like that. . . .

I have been lucky. . . . We have been married for nineteen years. We lived with my family for one month after we were married, then we came here. At first, I was excited about doing something new and different, but when I got here it was so difficult for me. I was so lonely. There was no one for me to talk to, nowhere for me to go. That was the worst part, being so lonely. (Anisa in Aswad, pp. 311–13)

What happened next . . .

In the late 1970s, after Anisa and her husband had settled in the United States, the number of Yemeni immigrants began to decrease. Many of the sojourners decided to work in other Middle Eastern countries. The 1991 Persian Gulf War (when the United States attacked Iraq after that country invaded Kuwait) disrupted life in the Middle East, however. More than 1.5 million Yemenis were driven out of the region by the war. The *Yemen Times* reported in 1997 that many of the sojourners who had returned from America to Yemen "sought to return to the states and some of them succeeded in going as visitors, and are still striving to adjust their legal status."

Did you know . . .

- Like her sons, Anisa's daughters are also interested in medicine. One wants to be a doctor, and the other wants to be a nurse.

- The largest communities of Yemeni Americans are found in the states of New York, Michigan, and California. In recent years, communities have been growing in Virginia, North Carolina, and South Carolina.

- Yemenis constitute one of the fastest-growing groups of Arab immigrants to the United States; 2,100 of them entered the country in 1992.

For More Information

Al-Ashwal, Shaker A. "Yemenis in America." *Yemen Times* (October 20–26, 1997). Available at http://www.yementimes.com/97/iss42/report.htm (March 1999).

Aswad, Barbara C., and Barbara Bilgé, eds. *Family and Gender among American Muslims: Issues Facing Middle Eastern Immigrants and Their Descendants*. Philadelphia: Temple University Press, 1996.

Shameem Rassam Amal

"Shameem Rassam Amal"
**Selection from *Bint Arab: Arab and Arab American Women in the United States*, by Evelyn Shakir
Published in 1997**

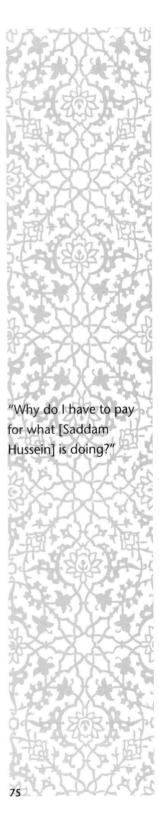

During the first twenty years of the third wave of Arab immigration, more than 40,000 people moved from Iraq to the United States (averaging 2,000 per year). The rate steadily increased; 7,400 Iraqis entered the United States in 1992.

"Why do I have to pay for what [Saddam Hussein] is doing?"

One of the reasons for Iraqi emigration was the eight-year war between Iraq and Iran that ended in 1988. More than 1,000,000 people died during that conflict (the two countries' total population was about 66,000,000). The poverty that resulted from the United Nations' refusal to allow Iraq to sell oil to other countries after that country invaded Kuwait in 1990 also encouraged emigration. (The United Nations is a world organization devoted to promoting peace among nations.) Without the income from oil sales, the Iraqi government could not pay its employees enough or buy food and medical supplies from other countries. More than 1,000,000 Iraqis left their starving country in the 1990s. Lack of food and medicine caused the deaths of 7,000 children under the age of five each month in Iraq, Denis Halliday, a United Nations observer, noted in a 1998 speech.

The brutal rule of Iraq's president, Saddam Hussein (1937–), was also a great factor in the wave of emigration from Iraq. When the United Nations placed economic sanctions on Iraq, limiting what it could import, including food and medicine, many of its members hoped that the Iraqi people would overthrow Hussein's government. "Saddam rules by a potent combination of terror and secrecy," Barbara Crossette wrote in 1998 in the *New York Times*. Crossette also reported that when Iraq held an election in 1995 to determine whether Hussein should remain president:

> in the days preceding the vote, [Hussein's political party] workers combed every neighborhood, going door to door to ask if the household had ration cards, a subtle message that the family's subsidized food might be in jeopardy if adults failed to vote. Rumors were deliberately circulated about the sophisticated methods the government had for detecting negative ballots, even if cast in secret.

It was this type of government intimidation that had an impact on Shameem Rassam Amal's life in Iraq and made her afraid to return from a visit to the United States.

Things to remember while reading "Shameem Rassam Amal":

- In many countries, television and radio stations, newspapers, and magazines are controlled by the government, which can decide what the people should be allowed to hear or see. In other countries, like the United States, the broadcast and print media are operated as private businesses that are free to transmit and publish what they wish, with little governmental interference.

- Saddam Hussein became the president of Iraq in 1979. He used his country's military forces to persecute minorities (especially the Kurdish people) inside Iraq and to attack neighboring countries. His actions resulted in hardships on the Iraqi people through wartime bombings and through restrictions on trade with other nations.

- In 1990, Hussein sent Iraq's army to take control of neighboring Kuwait, a wealthy, oil-producing country.

"Shameem Rassam Amal"

In **Baghdad**, we worked under machine guns because the radio and the TV stations were the most important facilities under government control. So we had the tanks there all the time and special units from the army. Radio and TV means control of everything. That's where you reach the remote places in Iraq if you overthrow the government. It's where you issue your first **communiqué.**

The director of television and radio would have his machine gun on his desk when I would go to his office. That's how they treated us.

You learn to survive, you don't want to see yourself in one of the jails; you don't want to see your family in one of the jails; you don't want to see your neighbors. So you don't argue politically, you don't tell people that you know better, you don't think.

In the studio, there's several telephones in front of the one who's in charge that night. This telephone is from the palace, this telephone is from the vice president, this is from the military security, this is from internal security.

Now this is what happens. A telephone rings. The man in the studio would do like this [rises to attention]. "Yes, sir!" And he's so scared he's almost going to urinate on himself. Then he runs. He doesn't even know what the caller said; all he remembers is it's the president's voice or vice president's or prime minister's and he said something about the show that's on the air right now. The man runs out, "Stop that show!" They stop it, just like that. Then whoever is doing that show, he's suspended from even appearing on TV, and nobody knows why.

That is what happened to me. I had a program. The prime minister calls in. He says, "Why is Shameem smiling so much?" For seven months I was suspended from being on the air. Then one day, my husband ran into the prime minister. The prime minister said, "How come I haven't seen Shameem for some time on TV?" My husband said, "Because of you. It seems you called the TV and made a comment." The prime minister said, "Oh no, I didn't mean to take her off the air. I just said she was smiling." My husband said, "I think you should make another call."

Baghdad: The capital of Iraq.

Communiqué: Announcement.

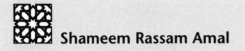

Shameem Rassam Amal

Shameem Rassam Amal grew up in Mosul, Iraq, although she spent her summers in Beirut, Lebanon, her mother's home city. Her mother was a teacher who spoke French and English in addition to her native Arabic. Compared to life in Lebanon, Amal found life difficult in Iraq. She remembers that her mother made their home seem like a safe, comfortable island of beauty. "My mother would insist, 'Come and look at the grass, come and look at the flower, feel it, touch it,'" Amal related to Evelyn Shakir, as quoted in *Bint Arab*. "And even when she was standing in the kitchen cooking, she would tell me, 'Come and see, come and touch.' That's the way I was taught to appreciate things as they are."

My mother and my husband were the people I trusted in my life. My husband was my first supporter, he pushed me a lot, he was my best friend. When he died, I lost somebody that I can talk to confidentially.

[During the Iran–Iraq War], the rockets would come or a missile would fall. Before an air raid, you would hear the alarm. What can you do? You can count, five to seven minutes, because that's the time it takes airplanes to cross the border and come to Baghdad. You learn where is the safest part of the house; you stand at the corner of two cement walls. I did that at first. Then after a while, I would go on with my daily chores. Out of nervousness, I would start cleaning the house or washing dishes. Even if they're clean dishes, I'll start washing them. All the time, I'm counting the minutes. When it's over, I thank God.

Once there was a big explosion, the radio station was attacked. It was a big **lorry** with dynamite—one of those suicides; he crashed himself into the building. It was around ten o'clock in the morning, we were having coffee, and then all of a sudden we heard the explosion. So the Civil Defense came to take us out of the buildings, and I remember we were standing in the courtyard, and the **Republican Guard** on the roofs of all the buildings had their guns aimed at us because they didn't know who's behind it. Then you see your **colleagues** coming out of the building, all in blood, and falling in front of you, and you cannot help them. You're not supposed to move. The soldiers are shouting at you, "Don't you ever move!"

My sister called me from the [United] States and said, "Why don't you come here for the summer?" A week after I was here, the war started with Kuwait. My brother said, "It's not wise for you to go back."

I heard there were several reports written about me back home, accusing me to be a traitor. I thought, "That's it, you're going to

Lorry: Truck.

Republican Guard: A unit of Iraqi soldiers.

Colleagues: Co-workers.

Political asylum: Permission to stay in a different country for protection from the government of one's home country.

stay." I was granted **political asylum.** Then I'm starting from scratch, I'm starting from no money. I had seven hundred dollars with me; I left everything else behind: my three houses, my cars, my money in the bank, my stock. I said, "Why do I have to pay for what that man [Saddam Hussein] is doing?"

I wanted my children to grow up in Iraq knowing my friends, knowing the back streets of every Arab country. I wanted my daughter to grow up to know what my culture is, my tradition as a woman. And maybe to have new ideas to improve that. I wanted my son and daughter to be close to their father's tomb, to visit it often. I wanted, myself, to see the palm trees growing in my backyard, to smell that odor of every day. I said, "Why do I have to give it up for that man? He has ruined my life." *(Amal in* Shakir, *pp. 171–73)*

Saddam Hussein (1937–), leader of Iraq beginning in 1979. Though Iraq cannot afford to repair electric plants and hospitals that were damaged during the Gulf War, Hussein is having the world's largest mosque built to increase his support among his own people.
Reproduced by permission of Archive Photos/Imapress.

What happened next . . .

Amal was afraid to return to Iraq after it invaded Kuwait. In 1991, a few months after that invasion, a United Nations military force led by the United States attacked Iraq and forced it to withdraw from Kuwait. The two-month-long conflict became known as the Persian Gulf War.

Did you know . . .

- According to the *New York Times,* in Iraq in January 1998 a doctor earned 3,000 dinars (Iraqi currency) a month. Two pounds of chicken cost about 1,000 dinars, and a dozen eggs cost 1,200 dinars.

- Because the government pays very low wages to professionals such as teachers and scientists, these highly educated people work an extra job or two, doing unskilled work like driving taxis. Many leave Iraq to work in other countries.

- Iraq cannot afford to repair electric plants, telephone systems, water distribution systems, and hospitals that were damaged during the Gulf War. Yet, in 1998, Hussein's government began constructing the world's largest mosque (Muslim house of worship), which will hold 45,000 people. He hopes this will increase his support among his own people and the governments of other Muslim nations.

For More Information

Crossette, Barbara. "Splendor and Ruin: The Tale of Two Baghdads." *New York Times,* January 31, 1998. Available at http://www.mtholyoke.edu/acad/intrel/coniraq.htm (March 1999).

Halliday, Denis. "Why I Resigned My UN Post in Protest of Sanctions." Speech delivered at Harvard University, November 5, 1998. Available at http://www.realtime.net/~liana/no_war/unresign.htm (March 1999).

Hamada, Tarek. "20,000 Chaldeans Eager for Life in America." *Arab American News,* July 2, 1993, pp. PG.

Shakir, Evelyn. *Bint Arab: Arab and Arab American Women in the United States.* Westport, CT: Praeger, 1997.

Mojahid Daoud

"Growing Up Arab in America"

**Selection from *Arab Americans: Continuity & Change*, edited by
Baha Abu-Laban and Michael W. Suleiman
Published in 1989**

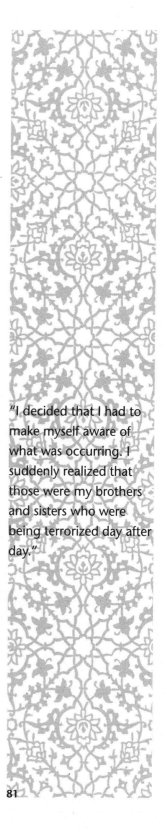

"I decided that I had to make myself aware of what was occurring. I suddenly realized that those were my brothers and sisters who were being terrorized day after day."

Mojahid Daoud's father immigrated to the United States from Jordan in 1952, four years after the United Nations, an international body established to promote world peace, established the nation of Israel. Israel had been created out of Palestinian Arab lands as a Jewish homeland. Almost immediately, war broke out between the Israelis and the neighboring Arabs, and more Arab territory was lost to the new nation. About 750,000 Palestinian Arabs were driven from Israel by force or fear, and many of them fled into neighboring Jordan. Although the United Nations provided some food and medical supplies for the refugees, the provisions did not meet their needs. Jordan accepted the refugees as new citizens and tried to help support them; that effort caused economic hardship throughout the country.

After working for several years in the United States, Daoud's father returned to Jordan to marry. A few years later he brought his wife and children back to America to escape the poverty that still plagued Jordan. As he grew up in Ohio, Daoud, who was born in Jordan around 1962, struggled to

Arab women and men receive their first allotment of blankets—one for every three persons—from the United Nations (UN) Palestine Relief Organization in July 1949, a year after the state of Israel was created on Palestinian land. Although the UN provided some food and medical supplies, the provisions did not meet the refugees' needs. These refugees were sheltered in tents just north of the Egyptian border. *Reproduced by permission of AP/Wide World Photos.*

figure out his personal identity. Was he an Arab or an American? Was it possible to be both?

Things to remember while reading "Growing Up Arab in America":

- Believing that private companies were making large profits while paying low prices for the oil their countries produced, a group of countries joined together in 1960 to form the Organization of Petroleum Exporting Countries (OPEC). They were poor countries (many, though not all, were Middle Eastern), and they decided that they could increase the price they received for their oil by agreeing on how much to produce: when the supply is small, buyers are willing to pay more. OPEC took its first decisive action in 1973 by increasing prices of crude (unprocessed) oil by 70 percent and refusing to sell oil to the

United States, the wealthiest large customer, because it had supported Israel in a war against its Arab neighbors.

- Abscam was an operation carried out by the Federal Bureau of Investigation (FBI) from 1978 to 1980. Suspecting that some members of the U.S. Congress were willing to take bribes, the FBI made up a company called Abdul Enterprises, Ltd., that was supposedly run by an Arab sheikh (chief of a tribe or clan). (The word "Abscam" was a contraction of "Abdul Scam.") One senator and six representatives were convicted of taking money from FBI agents posing as the sheikh and his employees and promising to help them in various ways, such as getting permission for the "sheikh" to enter the country and getting approval for gambling casinos. Videotapes of the "Arabs" paying the bribes to the congressmen were played on television news programs after the operation was finished. Despite the bribery convictions, many people thought the congressmen had been entrapped, or tricked into committing a crime they would not ordinarily have committed.

- The Palestine Liberation Organization (PLO), a military-type group formed to take Palestinian lands back from Israel, established its headquarters in Lebanon in 1970. Seeking to stop the PLO's terrorist attacks, Israel invaded Lebanon in 1982. The bloody invasion resulted in a three-year occupation of Lebanon by the Israeli army.

"Growing Up Arab in America"

*When I started elementary school my parents realized that the name Mojahid Daoud simply would not be appropriate for my early school years. The other kids would in all likelihood not learn how to pronounce the name and, even if they did (four or five pronunciations later), they would probably laugh at it. Or so we thought. Consequently, I was given Mark David as a school name—which was to remain my name throughout **adolescence**. It was not an **insignifi-***

Adolescence: Teenage years.

Insignificant: Minor.

cant change. I would not stand out as different from the other kids. This eventually served to lessen my identity as an Arab.

During those years, I never suffered any of the indignities that other Arab immigrants might suffer. I looked white, liked baseball, and did everything the other kids in school or on my block did. . . . My parents were always **cognizant** of the importance of not **alienating** their children from the American kids. If it meant **relinquishing** our identities as Arabs, they were willing to sacrifice that for our happiness. This was not easy for them. It was not as though their escape from the overwhelming poverty of Jordan led them to want to relinquish all **remnants** of their life there. They were very proud Arabs who had strong **familial** and religious ties to their country of birth. Despite their improved **lot** in the United States, America was to be only a vehicle by which they could return to Jordan and resume their lives there. . . .

However, despite my parents' strong ethnic pride and their attempts to make us proud Arabs, my brother and I rejected our heritage. We felt that we did not want to be different from Americans and that, if we **asserted** our identity, we would never be accepted. Furthermore, we felt that our Arab culture was backward compared to American culture. Our return to Jordan in 1972, supposedly to live there for good, only solidified these beliefs. We returned to a country so poor and **destitute**, having been wracked by a civil war, that we knew we would never make our home there. We went from playing kickball and swimming in our neighbor's pool to playing in open sewers and seeing lambs sacrificed before our eyes. It was too much for a child my age to cope with. We came back to the United States to resume our disrupted lives.

In many ways, our life back in the United States followed patterns similar to those in Jordan. My uncles and cousins all lived in the same neighborhood with us and we saw each other every day. We drank, ate, played, and even married together. It was as though the clan as well as our laws of social governance had been transplanted to Cincinnati [Ohio]. We were even locked together economically through a chain of restaurants in which our entire family was involved. This turned out to be a very important element in our collective identity: it provided an environment that in many ways was socially similar to the life back in **Fuheis**. With the exception of the world of school, we never really had to enter the larger society around us.

Cognizant: Aware.

Alienating: Setting apart.

Relinquishing: Giving up.

Remnants: Bits.

Familial: Family.

Lot: Fate; destiny.

Asserted: Strongly displayed; proclaimed.

Destitute: Needy.

Fuheis: Daoud's parents' home village in Jordan.

By the time I began high school, I was fully adjusted to American life. I had many friends and was fairly well known to all my classmates. I played football and was able to make the all-league first team as guard. At the same time, I felt more and more distant from my Arab past. I had no Arab friends and the ones that I did know did not understand my experiences. I just wanted to fit in with my classmates.

Nevertheless, I still knew my place in the school as an Arab. I was constantly referred to as sand-nigger and camel jockey, even by teachers that I knew. At the time, I just shrugged off the remarks because I thought that they were directed at me and not my culture. I just felt that the guys were joking around. I knew little of the political undertones that had produced this mindset.

*At that time (1973), the Arab oil **embargo** was **initiated** and everyone was under the impression that the Arabs had somehow devised a plot to bring about America's **demise** through the power of oil. This was reflected not only in the attitudes of my fellow students but in the popular culture as well. Many songs and films of the time discredited the culture and **integrity** of Arabs. The Abscam **fiasco** brought to the forefront just how far our politicians were willing to go in order to **denigrate** Arabs. . . .*

*Luckily, my family, including my extended family, was able to establish a thriving business in Cincinnati. It enabled us to bypass the difficult task of having to enter mainstream American society to find jobs. Nevertheless, our parents' alienation made them extremely **paranoid** of the outside world. . . .*

*I entered the University of Cincinnati in the fall of 1979. Things did not change much as far as my **orientation** to my ethnicity was concerned. I lived, ate, and drank with Americans, and they remained my only frame of reference for judging the world. I was having a great time American-style, and I was not about to change it. But that orientation was drastically altered with the Israeli invasion of Lebanon in 1982. Up until that time my political awareness was lacking, and I still faithfully believed in American politics. That, however, quickly dissolved after viewing, night after night, Israel's massive bombardment of Lebanon, with America's blessing. My human spirit was being tested as I realized that I could not sit idly by. I decided that I had to make myself aware of what was occurring. I suddenly realized that those were my brothers and sisters who were being terrorized day after day.*

Embargo: Ban on trade.

Initiated: Begun.

Demise: Death.

Integrity: Honesty; righteousness.

Fiasco: Ridiculous failure.

Denigrate: Belittle.

Paranoid: Suspicious.

Orientation: Position.

Mojahid Daoud

Born about 1962 in Fuheis, Jordan, Mojahid Daoud moved to the United States with his parents and his brother while he was very young. He did not see the differences between Jordan and America until his family moved back to Jordan when he was ten years old. A year later, they returned to Ohio, where Daoud's father and uncles owned a chain of restaurants.

Like many Arab immigrants, Daoud's father came to the United States with no money. He had been a tobacco farmer in Jordan, but in Ohio he began working as a peddler, selling linens (such as sheets and tablecloths) door to door. After three years of this work, he opened a small restaurant with his savings. His business was successful enough to allow him to support his parents and brothers in Jordan.

Palestinian cause: The desire of Palestinian Arabs to reclaim their land, which became the property of Israel.

Dimension: Component; major factor.

Compelled: Motivated.

Consciousness: Awareness; sense of one's self and one's purpose in life.

I started to get involved with the other Arabs at the university who were activists in the **Palestinian cause.** They became very close and proved to be good friends who would do just about anything for me. At the same time, I began to distance myself from my American friends who were still the way I once was, mainly interested in having a good time. . . . Obviously, people go through changes but this one I felt would be too much for my friends to handle. This was probably a mistake because ultimately I never gave my friends the chance to accept this new dramatic **dimension** in my life. . . .

In the summer following my graduation, I went back to Jordan to, as they say, rediscover myself. The first time I visited had been a terrible experience. We felt our parents were trying to take away something that we loved, namely our American identity. We could not understand what **compelled** my parents to want to return to Jordan. This time was different. Where the smell of goats and chickens had once offended me, it now became a cultural expression of our folklore. Where the simplicity of a farmer tilling the land with his oxen had appeared backward, it now seemed a romantic alternative to the mechanized, undefinable lifestyle of the United States. What I had really come to terms with was the fact that, in some way, I was witnessing myself and my past. I was not ashamed of it as I once was. I was proud to be from this naked land. . . .

Following my return from Palestine and Jordan, my **consciousness** was reshaped. I had developed a pride in my Arab past so great that I considered myself not an American, as I once did, but an Arab. Much was a result of my social relationships with other Arabs. However, my raised political consciousness was the most important reason why I began to change. Consequently, I began to take academics more seriously and decided to pursue a field where I might be *in the service of my fellow man. I enrolled in the urban planning program at the University of Michigan. . . .*

*For the first time, I was with other Arab Americans who talked, looked, and thought as I did. Although they were very small in number, they seemed to understand everything I had been through. They had had many American friends, yet they had become politically **galvanized.** I could see that they were even more confused than I had been. Many of them felt that it was necessary to maintain both identities. They did not want to give up their ethnic heritage, yet, at the same time, maintaining contact with American society was important for them. No one wants to feel as if they are not a part of the predominant student life. I knew from my experiences, however, that it is very difficult to maintain such a **posture** unless your American friends are open enough to accept your ethnic origins. . . .*

*As for me, I have finally stopped **deluding** myself as to who I am. Early in my life, it was so important for me to be accepted in this society as an American that I rejected my ancient heritage. Later on, as I became more politically conscious and aware of the beauty of traditional Arab life, it became important for me to be recognized as an Arab, to the point of even rejecting my American identity. In each instance, the feeling of alienation **impelled** me to choose one side, instead of **integrating** the two. I still ask myself why it is necessary to be forced to choose. (Daoud in Abu-Laban, pp. 174–79)*

What happened next . . .

Daoud visited Jordan and embraced his Arab roots in the early 1980s. In 1988, in order to create a new country of Palestine, Jordan gave up its claim to the West Bank of the River Jordan. Israel, however, had taken control of the disputed territory during a war in 1967 and it continued to hold it through the 1990s, building new settlements among the Palestinian refugee camps there. On and off throughout the 1990s the landless Palestinian government and the Israeli government have tried to agree on terms for a transfer of control of the land.

Galvanized: Energized.

Posture: Position.

Deluding: Deceiving; fooling.

Impelled: Forced.

Integrating: Combining.

Did you know . . .

- During the early 1990s, Jordanians accounted for one-sixth of the Arabs entering the United States, ranking behind only Lebanese and Egyptians.

- Among metropolitan areas with the largest population of Arab Americans, the Los Angeles-Long Beach area of southern California ranks third. About 50,000 Jordanian Americans live there.

- Since 1946, Jordan has been a kingdom ruled by members of the Hashemite family. When King Hussein died in 1999, he had held the throne for forty-seven years. He chose his eldest son, Abdullah, to follow him as king.

For More Information

Daoud, Mojahid. "Growing Up Arab in America." *Arab Americans: Continuity & Change,* edited by Baha Abu-Laban and Michael W. Suleiman. Belmont, MA: Association of Arab-American University Graduates, 1989.

El-Badry, Samia. "The Arab-American Market." *American Demographics,* January 1994. Available at www.demographics.com/publications/ad/94_ad/9401_ad/ad505.htm (February 1999).

Arab Americans,
Civil Rights, and Prejudice

A stereotype is an image, trait, or mode of behavior that is inappropriately applied to all individuals who share a common religion, sex, ethnic origin, geographic location, political party, socio-economic bracket, or other [noticeable] factor that may set them apart from others," wrote Marsha J. Hamilton in "The Arab Woman in U.S. Popular Culture: Sex and Stereotype." Various groups of immigrants have faced stereotyping and prejudice after they came to America.

Arab immigrants have many characteristics that make them an easy target for stereotyping. Their skin color and facial features are distinctive. Their native language contains sounds that are unfamiliar to English speakers. Some Arabs wear exotic clothing like kaffiyehs (kuh-FEE-yuhs), a cloth head covering secured with a cord wrapped around the head. Many recent Arab immigrants are Muslims, and the Muslim religion, Islam, is poorly understood in the United States.

Like other immigrants in the nineteenth century, Arabs faced prejudice in America. The Chinese Exclusion Act of 1882 refused permission for Chinese people to settle in the United States, and in 1899 an Associated Charities of Boston

Arab American men wearing kaffiyehs. Arab immigrants have many characteristics that make them easy targets for stereotyping, including wearing traditional clothing. *Reproduced by permission of AP/Wide World Photos.*

report stated: "Next to the Chinese, who can never be in any real sense Americans, the Syrians are the most foreign of all foreigners." As quoted in *An Ancient Heritage: The Arab-American Minority,* the report continued, "Whether on the street in their Oriental costumes or in their rooms gathered around the Turkish pipe, they are always apart from us . . . and out of all nationalities would be distinguished for nothing whatever excepting as curiosities." **Michael Shadid,** who came to the United States from Syria in 1898, encountered so much prejudice while he was working as a peddler (door-to-door salesman) that he tried to change his name when he applied to medical school. After he became a doctor and introduced ways to make medical care more affordable, other doctors who felt threatened by his revolutionary ideas used Shadid's ethnicity as one way of attacking him.

After World War I (1914–18), Americans became even more concerned about allowing foreigners from unfamiliar cultures to move into the United States. The National Origins

Act of 1924 limited the number of immigrants each year from most countries to 2 percent of the number of people from that country who had been living in the United States in 1890. By basing those quotas (limits) on 1890, the U.S. government made sure there would only be a few immigrants from places other than northern and western Europe, from where most of America's earlier immigrants had come. Country-based limits on immigration continued until 1965. After that time, Arabs and Arab Americans began to face a different kind of prejudice.

As more Arabs, many of them Muslims, entered the United States under the 1965 immigration law, their increasing numbers and distinctive characteristics drew greater attention to them as a group. A series of Middle Eastern wars and terrorist incidents involving Arabs or Muslims made much of that attention negative. (A terrorist is a person who uses violence or threats to frighten or intimidate a group or government into giving in to the terrorist's demands, usually political.) Not only did Arab Americans face informal prejudice and suspicion, but they also became the targets of selective government laws that threatened their civil rights. As one of the groups targeted for electronic surveillance (wiretaps and hidden microphones), Arabs in America were directly affected by the **Foreign Intelligence Surveillance Act of 1978.** Later, they became practically the only group in the United States impacted by some parts of the **Antiterrorism and Effective Death Penalty Act of 1996.**

Since the mid-1960s, Arab Americans have formed many organizations that educate the public, challenge unequal enforcement of the law, and encourage their community to speak out about discrimination and prejudice. **Magdoline Asfahani**, a college student, spoke out by writing to *Newsweek* magazine about her experiences. **Ghassan Saleh**, a Muslim engineer, spoke out by writing a column in the *Dallas Morning News*. **Zana Macki**, who has been active in the American-Arab Anti-Discrimination Committee, the Arab Community Center for Economic and Social Services, and the Muslim American Alliance, makes speeches and writes newspaper columns. As the executive director of the American Muslim Council, **Atif Harden** offered his thoughts and suggestions to a U.S. House of Representatives committee that was considering how to fight international terrorism, which many people associate with Arabs or Muslims, although members of other groups commit more terrorist acts.

For More Information

Ashabranner, Brent. *An Ancient Heritage: The Arab-American Minority.* New York: HarperCollins, 1991.

Deep, Said. "Rush to Judgment (Blaming Muslims for Terrorist Attacks)." *The Quill,* July–August 1995, pp. 18 ff.

Hamilton, Marsha J. "The Arab Woman in U.S. Popular Culture: Sex and Stereotype." In *Food for Our Grandmothers: Writings by Arab-American and Arab-Canadian Feminists.* Edited by Joanna Kadi. Boston: South End Press, 1994, pp. 173–80.

Said, Edward W. *Covering Islam: How the Media and the Experts Determine How We See the Rest of the World.* New York: Vintage Books, 1997.

United States Government

Foreign Intelligence Surveillance Act of 1978
Antiterrorism and Effective Death Penalty Act of 1996

The 1967 Six Day War between Arab and Israeli forces caused a marked increase in anger and suspicion toward Arab Americans from other Americans, and from government agencies. Still upset about the loss of Arab land due to the founding of Israel in 1948 (it was established on Palestinian land), Egypt had blocked one of Israel's main ports and gathered troops near the Israeli border. Expecting to be attacked, Israel struck first, destroying the Egyptian air force and capturing land from Egypt, Syria, and Jordan in the brief but fierce war. The United States Government and most Americans supported Israel's existence—it was founded as a homeland for Jews after decades of persecution in Europe and Asia—so when the conflict erupted, they considered Arabs the enemy. Individual Arab Americans were insulted or challenged to explain the actions of Arab governments, something many of them knew little about. The Federal Bureau of Investigation (FBI) and other government agencies responsible for national security became increasingly suspicious of Arabs and Arab Americans.

"An alien subject to removal under this title shall not be entitled to suppress evidence that the alien alleges was unlawfully obtained."

Lebanese Americans protesting in Washington, D.C., 1996. Muslims and Arab Americans are subjected to a high rate of surveillance. *Reproduced by permission of AP/Wide World Photos.*

Coincidentally, 1967 was also the year the U.S. Supreme Court decided that electronic surveillance (for example, wiretaps and hidden microphones) was a kind of search outlawed by the Fourth Amendment to the Constitution, which protects against unreasonable search and seizure. Before that, the government had been free to eavesdrop electronically on anyone. The Supreme Court's decision meant that, like a physical search of a person's home or office, an electronic search would require a court order. To get the order, law-enforcement agents would have to convince a judge that there was good reason to suspect the person of illegal activity. The only exception was in the area of national security: the Supreme Court decision left open the possibility that the government might not have to get a court order for electronic surveillance that was necessary to protect the American government.

In response to the Supreme Court decision, Congress passed the Omnibus Crime Control and Safe Streets Act in 1968. This law established procedures for state and federal police to get court permission for using electronic surveillance to investigate crimes. The U.S. attorney general, under direction of the president, continued to authorize electronic surveillance for national-security purposes without court orders; in these cases, the government was not investigating crimes but was trying to gather intelligence information (in a sense, spying).

By 1978, Congress had become concerned that the government was bending the rules, claiming that it needed wiretaps for national security when it actually wanted them for other reasons. For example, rather than having to persuade a judge that there was already enough evidence to authorize a wiretap, an agency such as the FBI could simply ask the National Security Agency (NSA) for help. The NSA could install a wiretap without a court order, supposedly for national-security purposes, and then turn over any crime evidence it found to the FBI. To try and limit this abuse, Congress passed the Foreign Intelligence Surveillance Act of 1978 (FISA). This law created procedures for the government to obtain court orders for electronic surveillance of U.S. citizens for reasons of national security. FISA also included procedures allowing the government to use electronic surveillance on noncitizens in the United States without a court order.

During the 1960s and 1970s, federal agencies suspected several groups of trying to undermine the government—especially civil-rights activists (like Martin Luther King Jr. [1929–1968]), protesters against the Vietnam War (1965–75, when U.S. forces tried to keep communist North Vietnam from taking over noncommunist South Vietnam), and Arabs. Besides the Six Day War, several other highly publicized events fueled the suspicions toward Arabs. For example, Palestinian extremists hijacked at least six passenger planes between 1970 and 1977, and eleven Israeli athletes and five Palestinian terrorists were killed in a hostage situation at the 1972 Olympic Games in Munich, Germany. From 1972 until 1974, in what he called an attempt to protect American Jews and Israeli visitors from possible terrorist attacks, President Richard M. Nixon (1913–1994) ordered the FBI and other agencies to investigate Arab Americans and other Arabs in the United States.

For the next twenty-five years, various civil rights and Arab American organizations complained that Muslim and Arab visitors, residents, and citizens of the United States were subjected to a higher rate of surveillance and deportation (being sent back to their native countries) than other ethnic groups. Although they did not specifically mention Arabs or Muslims, some laws were enforced more actively against them than against other groups or individuals. One such law was the Antiterrorism and Effective Death Penalty Act of 1996 (AEDPA), which allowed the government to deport people on the basis of secret evidence. The evidence can be kept secret even from the defendants and their attorneys—which makes it impossible for them to defend themselves properly. Two years after AEDPA was passed, the *New York Times* reported that secret evidence was currently being used against twenty-five people, all of whom were either Muslim or were of Arab ancestry.

Things to remember while reading FISA and AEDPA:

- Among other things, the First Amendment to the U.S. Constitution guarantees that no law can limit people's right to say what they believe or to attend peaceful gatherings. The U.S. Supreme Court has ruled that contributing money to a political organization is protected by the First Amendment because it is an expression of opinion, showing agreement with the organization's goals.

- The Fourth Amendment to the U.S. Constitution says that the police cannot search anyone (or their property) unless they get specific permission by convincing a judge that there is a strong reason to suspect the person of wrongdoing.

Foreign Intelligence Surveillance Act of 1978

The text of this document has been abridged.

Section 102(a)(1) **Notwithstanding** *any other law, the President, through the Attorney General, may authorize* **electronic surveillance** *without a* **court order** *under this Act to* **acquire** *foreign intelligence information for periods of up to one year if there is no substantial likelihood that the surveillance will acquire the contents of any communication to which a* **United States person** *is a party.*

Section 102(b) A judge to whom an application [for a court order] is made may, notwithstanding any other law, grant an order approving electronic surveillance of a foreign power or an agent of a foreign power for the purpose of obtaining foreign intelligence information if such surveillance may involve the acquisition of communications of any United States person and the application meets the other conditions described in this Act.

Section 103(a) The Chief **Justice** *of the United States shall publicly* **designate** *seven district court judges from seven of the United States judicial circuits who shall* **constitute** *a court which shall have* **jurisdiction** *to hear applications for and grant orders approving electronic surveillance anywhere within the United States under the procedures set forth in this Act.*

Section 103(b) The Chief Justice shall publicly designate three judges from the United States district courts or courts of appeals, who together shall **comprise** *a court of review which shall have jurisdiction to review the denial of any application made under this Act.*

Section 105(a) Upon an application made according to the procedures described in this Act, the judge shall enter an **ex parte** *order as requested or as modified approving the electronic surveillance if he finds that there is* **probable cause** *to believe that the target of the electronic surveillance is a foreign power or an agent of a foreign power:* Provided, *That no United States person may be considered a foreign power or an agent of a foreign power solely upon the basis of activities protected by the first amendment to the Constitution of the United States.*

Notwithstanding: Regardless of.

Electronic surveillance: Using wiretaps and hidden microphones to collect evidence of a crime.

Court order: Permission from a judge, who must deem the reason for surveillance justified.

Acquire Gather; obtain.

United States person: A U.S. citizen or an alien (noncitizen) legally living as a permanent resident of the United States.

Justice: Judge.

Designate: Appoint.

Constitute: Make up; embody.

Jurisdiction: Authority.

Comprise: Make up, embody.

Ex parte: From one side only; that is, without the defendants or their attorneys being present.

Probable cause: Reasonable grounds for believing a charge is well-founded.

*Section 105(d) At or before the end of the period of time for which electronic surveillance is approved by an order or an extension, the judge may review the circumstances under which information concerning United States persons was acquired, **retained**, or **disseminated**.*

Section 108(a) On a semiannual basis the Attorney General shall fully inform the House Permanent Select Committee on Intelligence and the Senate Select Committee on Intelligence concerning all electronic surveillance conducted under this Act.

Antiterrorism and Effective Death Penalty Act of 1996

The text of this document has been abridged.

Section 302(a)(1)

*The Secretary [of State] is authorized to designate an organization as a foreign **terrorist** organization if the Secretary finds that (A) the organization is a foreign organization; (B) the organization engages in terrorist activity; and (C) the terrorist activity of the organization threatens the security of United States **nationals** or the national security of the United States.*

Section 303(a)

*Whoever, within the United States or subject to the **jurisdiction** of the United States, knowingly provides material support or resources to a foreign terrorist organization, or attempts or **conspires** to do so, shall be fined under this title or imprisoned not more than 10 years, or both.*

In any civil proceeding under this section, upon request made ex parte *and in writing by the United States, a court, upon a sufficient showing, may authorize the United States to (i) **redact** specified items of **classified** information from documents to be introduced into evidence or made available to the defendant; (ii) substitute a summary of the information for such classified documents; or (iii) substitute a statement admitting relevant facts that the classified information would tend to prove. If the court enters an order granting a request under this paragraph, the entire text of the documents to which the request relates shall be **sealed** and preserved in the records of the court to be made available to the **appellate court** in the event of an appeal. The court shall grant a request under this*

Retained: Held.

Disseminated: Distributed.

Terrorist: A person who uses violence or threats to frighten or intimidate a group or government into giving in to the terrorist's demands, usually political.

Nationals: Persons associated with a certain country.

Jurisdiction: Government.

Conspires: Plans.

Redact: Edit.

Classified: Available only to people who are given permission by the government.

Sealed: Secret.

Appellate court: Court of appeals.

*paragraph if the court finds that the redacted item, **stipulation**, or summary is sufficient to allow the defendant to prepare a defense.*

Section 401

*The Chief Justice of the United States shall publicly designate five district court judges from five of the United States judicial circuits who shall constitute a court that shall have jurisdiction to conduct all removal proceedings. In any case in which the Attorney General has classified information that an **alien** is an alien terrorist, the Attorney General may seek removal of the alien by filing an application with the removal court. An application under this section shall be submitted* ex parte *and **in camera,** and shall be filed under seal with the removal court.*

*A removal hearing shall be conducted under this section as **expeditiously** as practicable for the purpose of determining whether the alien to whom the order pertains should be removed from the United States on the grounds that the alien is an alien terrorist. The removal hearing shall be open to the public. An alien who is the subject of a removal hearing shall be given reasonable notice of (1) the nature of the charges against the alien, including a general account of the basis for the charges; and (2) the time and place at which the hearing will be held.*

*Discovery of information **derived pursuant to** the Foreign Intelligence Surveillance Act of 1978 or otherwise collected for national security purposes, shall not be authorized if **disclosure** would present a risk to the national security of the United States; an alien subject to removal under this title shall not be entitled to **suppress** evidence that the alien **alleges** was unlawfully obtained.*

The judge shall examine, ex parte *and* in camera, *any evidence for which the Attorney General determines that public disclosure would pose a risk to the national security of the United States or to the security of any individual because it would disclose classified information. With respect to such information, the Government shall submit to the removal court an unclassified summary of the specific evidence that does not pose that risk. Not later than fifteen days after submission, the judge shall approve the summary if the judge finds that it is sufficient to enable the alien to prepare a defense. The Government shall deliver to the alien a copy of the unclassified summary.*

Stipulation: Admission that certain facts are true.

Alien: Noncitizen.

In camera: In the judge's chamber; in private; in secret.

Expeditiously: Promptly.

Derived: Obtained.

Pursuant to: According to.

Disclosure: Making something known; revealing something.

Suppress: Keep hidden.

Alleges: Claims.

What happened next . . .

Five years after FISA became law in 1978, *The Nation* published an article by Herman Schwartz, a law professor at American University, titled "How Do We Know FISA Is Working?" Among other things, FISA required the Justice Department to report to Congress about how the law was being applied. Here are some of Schwartz's observations:

- Between 1978 and 1983, judges authorized nearly 1,500 electronic acts of surveillance under FISA. They did not deny a single government request.

- Even though FISA required the Justice Department to report to certain committees in the Senate and the House of Representatives twice a year, one member of the specified Senate committee said it had never discussed how well the law was working.

- Another member reported that the Senate committee never looked at specific cases to determine whether the government's applications and the judges' orders met the law's requirements. The appropriate House committee did look at a sample of cases and was satisfied that they met the terms of the law.

- George L. Hart Jr., who served as the first chief judge of the special court authorized by FISA, reported that the judges of the special court do not supervise the use of wiretaps and bugs they approve, even though the law authorizes them to do so. Therefore, they do not know whether the FISA limits are being obeyed.

One of the most controversial elements of the 1996 AEDPA allows the government to use secret evidence in certain cases. The law states that secret evidence will be used only if it is necessary for national security, that it must be evaluated by a judge, and that the defendants must be provided with a summary that gives them enough information to prepare a defense. However, there have been reports of apparent abuses. For example:

- The Interreligious Foundation for Community Organization (IFCO) reported in March 1998 that a federal immigration court ruled, based on secret evidence, that six Iraqis could be forced to leave the United States. "The judge issued a ninety-two-page decision, most of which also was kept from the six men and their lawyers, rendering an appeal a hideous joke," according to IFCO. One of the men's attorneys told the *New York Times,* "We never knew what was in the record [the evidence], we never knew what the case was about, and we still don't know."

- "Pieces of secret evidence have come out over the past year, pried loose by increasing political pressure or court orders," the *St. Petersburg Times* reported on October 4, 1998. "What [the public] has seen, critics say, is not evidence at all, but accusations that would not stand up in any U.S. court." The article quoted a well-known attorney who has represented defendants in half a dozen secret-evidence cases, saying that he has not seen "a shred of evidence that any of these individuals was engaged in any illegal activity."

- In a 1997 deportation case involving Egyptian Nassar Ahmed, who had lived in the United States for ten years, the Immigration and Naturalization Service (INS) offered only a summary of its secret evidence. According to a February 2, 1998, article in the *Detroit Free Press,* "The summary contained a list of nonconfidential biographical facts and a brief statement that the evidence included 'information concerning [Ahmed's] association with a known terrorist organization' which was not named. The judge called the summary 'largely useless.' In September 1999, an immigration judge ordered the release of Ahmed, who had already spent three years in jail on the basis of secret evidence. The following month, an immigration court of appeals ordered the release of Hany Kiareldeen, who had been imprisoned for eighteen months based on secret evidence. Both men remained in jail, however, while the INS appealed these decisions. According to an American-Arab Anti-Discrimination Committee press release dated October 19, 1999, "There are at least 20 individuals currently being held in jail in the United States without charge and on the basis of secret evidence. All of these prosecutions target immigrants of Arab descent."

Did you know . . .

- AEDPA's authorization of secret evidence is highly unusual in American law. Secret evidence cannot be used in criminal cases, including spy trials involving national security.

- In June 1999, the U.S. House of Representatives began considering a bill that would repeal the secret evidence provisions of the AEDPA.

For More Information

"ADC Congratulates Hany Kiareldeen on Victory over Secret Evidence." Available at www.adc.org/press/1999/19Oct99.htm (October 21, 1999).

Aschoff, Susan. "At Last Unveiled, Evidence Falls Short." *St. Petersburg Times* (Florida), October 4, 1998. Available at http://www.sptimes.com/Worldandnation/100498/At_last_unveiled_evi.html (October 20, 1999).

"Editorial: Secret Evidence?" *The Detroit News,* July 26, 1998. Available at http://detnews.com/EDITPAGE/9807/26/2edit/2edit.htm (October 20, 1999).

Krodel, Beth. "In a Nation That Promises Justice for All, Immigrants Who Haven't Committed Crimes are Imprisoned Based on Evidence That No One Can See: America's Captives." *Detroit Free Press,* February 2, 1998, p. 1A. Available at http://www.cafearabica.com/law/law captives12.html (October 20, 1999).

"National Coalition to Protect Political Freedom: UPDATE." Background paper issued by the National Coalition to Protect Political Freedom, a project of the Interreligious Foundation for Community Organization (IFCO), March 27, 1998. Available at http://www.ifconews.org/ncppf398.html (October 20, 1999).

Schwartz, Herman. "How Do We Know FISA Is Working?" *The Nation,* October 29, 1983, pp. 397–99.

Smothers, Ronald. "U.S. Bars or Expels Suspect Immigrants on Secret Evidence." *New York Times,* August 15, 1998, p. A1.

Michael A. Shadid

Crusading Doctor: My Fight for Cooperative Medicine
Excerpt from the memoirs of Michael A. Shadid
Published in 1956

Michael A. Shadid faced prejudice and discrimination in two ways. Some people simply mistrusted him because he looked foreign. Others disliked or feared his unusual ideas about health care and used ethnic prejudice to attack him.

During his childhood in a poor Syrian village, Shadid (1882–1966) saw the terrible consequences of inadequate health care. Eventually he immigrated to the United States and became a doctor, practicing medicine in Oklahoma farming communities. In America during the first half of the twentieth century, when Shadid practiced, health insurance was not widely available. Many people could not afford to go to a doctor until they were seriously ill. By then, they needed extensive care, which was often so expensive that it took them years to repay the debt; sometimes they even had to sell their homes to pay the doctor and hospital. Shadid thought it would be better for them to pay a manageable amount each year in exchange for routine medical care that would prevent many serious illnesses. He invented a system that he called "cooperative medicine," which was an early version of what is now known as managed care.

"Since the campaign against me did not at any time mention cooperative medicine or health insurance, but was devoted to socialism, communism, and my foreign birth, I resorted to the use of sarcasm and humor."

A Syrian man peddles food to a couple of customers on the streets of New York in the early twentieth century. After coming to the United States, Michael A. Shadid worked as a peddler to earn enough money to bring his mother and brother over and to finance his college and medical school education. *Reproduced by permission of Corbis Corporation (Bellevue).*

Many doctors felt threatened by Shadid's revolutionary approach to health care. They did not want to change the way they worked, and they were afraid that competition from Shadid would put them out of business. Throughout his career, Shadid faced strong opposition from groups ranging in size and prominence from his local medical society to the American Medical Association (AMA), a powerful, national organization of doctors. He faced informal "smear" campaigns designed to drive away his patients; his life was even threatened. And he faced formal efforts to take away his medical license and deny him essential malpractice insurance.

Shadid refused to surrender to the prejudices he faced because of his ethnicity and because of his boldness in challenging the established medical system. His dedication and hard work brought affordable health care to his home community, and his ideas spread throughout his professional community. By the mid-1950s, seventy-nine cooperative health programs in the United States and Canada served more than one million patients.

Things to remember while reading *Crusading Doctor: My Fight for Cooperative Medicine:*

- After World War II (1939–45), a strong rivalry called the Cold War (1946–89) developed between two opposite types of government. The United States was the leader of the "free world," which consisted of capitalist countries in which people could own their own land and businesses and choose their political leaders. The Union of Soviet Socialist Republics (USSR; the Soviet Union) led the communist nations, in which governments owned and controlled all property and businesses so that, in theory, they could distribute the profits equally to all its citizens. In actuality, the governments confiscated people's lands and were also known to severely punish citizens who disagreed with government policies, policies into which they had little input. Tensions were very high during this rivalry: being accused of being a communist was a serious charge that could destroy an American citizen's reputation and career.

- Socialism is also a political and economic system in which the government owns and controls all businesses. The United States is a capitalist country; however, some government programs could be considered socialist. Shadid thought this was true of President Franklin D. Roosevelt's (1882–1945) New Deal programs, for example, which gave government support to businesses and to individual citizens.

- In 1940, Shadid ran for election to the U.S. House of Representatives in the hopes of passing laws that would encourage cooperative medicine. He faced bitter opposition, which he described in *Crusading Doctor: My Fight for Cooperative Medicine.* His opponents spread many false rumors about him; for example, they said that if he were elected he would recommend only Syrians for appointment to public office, and they claimed he had murdered one of his daughters for marrying an American.

Crusading Doctor:
My Fight for Cooperative Medicine
1908–1940

In Stecker [Oklahoma] and in Oklahoma City I met with preju-
dice. I could not, if I wanted to, deny my foreign birth, as my **swarthy**
complexion and my **physiognomy** *plainly enough betrayed my origin.*
What could I do about it? I had two choices: I could go to some city in
the North or East where my foreign birth would not count against me,
or I could go to some medical center and learn to do things that the
average country doctor could not do, and then locate in a small town.
The first choice would take me too far away from my mother, brother,
and sister who lived on a farm in southwestern Oklahoma; and fur-
thermore, my finances were too low to buck the severe competition I
would meet within a city. I chose the latter course. . . .

In Carter [Oklahoma], my practice was largely among the farm-
ers. Some of the town friends of Dr. Danby [the other local doctor]
called me "The Jew Doctor" to emphasize the fact that I was a for-
eigner, though they did not know enough to distinguish between a
Hebrew and a Syrian. Dr. Danby did all he could **surreptitiously** *to*
discredit me. He knew a number of old women, **notorious** *gossips,*
in various parts of the surrounding community, to whom he whis-
pered [false] items which he knew they would soon spread. . . .

The report that I was a Jew led one of the doctors of nearby
Sayre [Oklahoma] to visit me. When I explained patiently that I was
not a Jew but a Christian, the doctor exclaimed, "Well, if you are not
a Jew, your mother certainly must have had a good look at one.". . .

[During a 1940 campaign for Congress:]

Since the campaign against me did not at any time mention co-
operative medicine or health insurance, but was devoted to **social-**
ism, **communism**, *and my foreign birth, I resorted to the use of sar-*
casm and humor, about as follows:

> *Ladies and Gentlemen: Before getting to the* **kernel**
> *of this talk let me blow away some of the* **chaff** *my extin-*
> *guished opponents have stirred up in this campaign*
> *against me. I say extinguished opponent because from*

Swarthy: Dark, olive.

Physiognomy: Facial features.

Surreptitiously: Secretly.

Notorious: Widely
recognized.

Socialism: A political system
in which the means of
producing and distributing
goods are shared by the
community or owned by the
government.

Communism: An economic
system that promotes the
ownership of most property
and means of production by
the community as a whole.

Kernel: Heart, core.

Chaff: Empty shell.

what I can make out, all nine of them have already agreed there is only one man in the race and that's me.

Well then, the first charge my united opponents make is that I am a Socialist. I deny the allegation. I used to be one but when the **New Deal** adopted my **platform** I had no other choice than either to go with it or to desert my convictions; so now I am a New Deal Democrat, or to be precise I was one long before the New Deal was known.

The second charge is that I am a Communist and in proof thereof they declare that sometime ago I was **cited** before a legislative committee to prove that I was not a Communist. Well I appeared before the honorable body in company with some twenty college professors and ministers of the gospel, and from what I read in the Oklahoma City papers it seems that the committee decided that while it might be all right to investigate a red-hot horse-shoe it would be **plumb** foolish to pick it up and put it in the pocket for future reference [that is, the committee investigated the charges and was satisfied enough to close the investigation].

The third charge is that I wasn't born in this country. And here my extinguished opponents "really **got the goods** on me." However, there are some **mitigating** circumstances that should be mentioned. In the first place when I was born, some 120 miles from where Christ was born, I was too young and inexperienced to know enough about geography to instruct my parents where I wanted to be born. However, in the event of my election I solemnly promise to do better next time.

Perhaps I also may add that when I came to this country at the age of 16 I was already able to read, write, and speak fluent English, all of which the bulk of my distinguished opponents still have to learn if judged by their vocal and literary utterances. Furthermore, when I came to this country I had clothes on my back whereas they arrived stark naked. (Shadid, Crusading Doctor, pp. 40, 49, 197–99)

New Deal: Series of programs instituted by U.S. president Franklin D. Roosevelt in the 1930s to lift America out of the Great Depression by providing incentives to businesses and jobs for the working classes.

Platform: Policies.

Cited: Summoned to explain myself.

Plumb: Absolutely.

Got the goods: Found the truth.

Mitigating: Excusing.

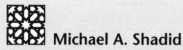 **Michael A. Shadid**

By the time Michael A. Shadid (1882–1966) was born in Judaidah, Syria, his father and nine of his eleven older brothers and sisters had died. The primitive village had no sewer system, so diseases spread easily. The villagers were poor, and many died of malnutrition. At the age of eleven, Shadid moved with his mother, brother, and sister to Beirut, Lebanon. His family all worked so that he, the youngest, could go to school. Shadid took full advantage of this great opportunity, completing high school in only three years.

Shadid attended an American high school in Beirut, where he learned English and American customs—he even played on the football team. Several of Shadid's relatives lived in New York, and he and his sister moved there in 1898. After working as a peddler (door-to-door salesman) for two years, Shadid was able to bring his mother and brother to the United States. After two more years of peddling, Shadid went to college and then medical school. From 1906 until 1946, he practiced medicine in Oklahoma. After he retired, Shadid traveled around the United States and Brazil asking for donations from Syrian immigrants to build a hospital in Judaidah in the newly independent country of Lebanon. When he had raised enough money, Shadid went back to his hometown to supervise construction of the hospital.

What happened next . . .

Shadid was one of ten candidates in his district's 1940 congressional primary election. He finished in second place, behind the incumbent (current) congressman. A few months later, that congressman died, and Shadid again ran for election. Once more, he finished in second place, losing by fewer than five hundred votes. Although he believed the ballots were counted dishonestly to keep him from victory, he was not able to prove it.

Did you know . . .

- During his peddling days in the northeastern United States, Shadid encountered a significant amount of prejudice against foreigners. Hoping to sidestep that problem, he used the name Michael Shade when he applied to medical school. One of his teachers persuaded him to keep his Arabic name.

• In 1959, George Kasem (1919–) became the first Lebanese American to serve in Congress, in the House of Representatives. In 1973, James Abourezk (AB-oor-ezk; 1931–) became the first Lebanese American senator.

For More Information

Shadid, Michael A. *Crusading Doctor: My Fight for Cooperative Medicine.* Norman, OK: University of Oklahoma Press, 1992.

Shadid, Michael A. *A Doctor for the People: The Autobiography of the Founder of America's First Co-operative Hospital.* New York: Vanguard Press, 1939.

Ghassan Saleh and Tom Quigley

"Blaming Bombing on Muslims Shows Prevalence of Prejudice"

Dallas Morning News guest column
Published May 13, 1995

On April 19, 1995, a truck containing a 4,800-pound bomb exploded in front of an Oklahoma City, Oklahoma, building that housed U.S. government offices and a day-care center. The explosion severely damaged the building, killing 168 people (including 15 children) and injuring 600 others.

One witness reported seeing two men "of possible Middle Eastern descent" running away from the building just before the explosion. Television, radio, and newspaper reports promptly broadcast this description. Many people who were searching for an explanation and looking for someone to blame for the horrible tragedy quickly assumed that Arab terrorists were responsible. (A terrorist is a person who uses violence or threats to frighten or intimidate a group or government into giving in to the terrorist's demands, usually political.) Over the next three days, more than two hundred episodes of anti-Arab or anti-Muslim hostility occurred around the United States, including verbal insults, threatening telephone calls, property damage, beatings, and shootings.

"Within twenty minutes of the first announcement that 'Middle Eastern men' had been seen outside of the federal building, the Dallas mosques began to receive threats. . . . . There was a quick and thoughtful response by the Muslim community. Instead of rightful anger, they went to work."

The Alfred P. Murrah Federal Building in Oklahoma City, Oklahoma, after it was bombed on April 19, 1995, killing 168 people and injuring 600 others. The bombing at first was believed to be the work of Arab terrorists. *Reproduced by permission of AP/Wide World Photos.*

Only hours after the bombing, authorities arrested Timothy McVeigh, a white American with no connection to Arabs or Muslims. On April 19, 1993, the U.S. government had ended a fifty-one-day standoff by attacking the compound of a religious group that was stockpiling weapons outside Waco, Texas. Deeply troubled by the deaths of eighty-one men, women, and children in that attack, McVeigh retaliated by bombing the government building exactly two years later. McVeigh was eventually convicted of the crime and was sentenced to death. Another non-Arab American, Terry Nichols, was convicted of helping with the bombing and was sentenced to life in prison with no possibility of parole.

Four weeks after the Oklahoma City bombing, two religious leaders—one Muslim and one Christian—spoke out to counter the anti-Arab and anti-Muslim sentiment that had erupted in their community. Ghassan Saleh was the general manager of the Islamic Association of North Texas, and Reverend Tom Quigley was the executive director of the Greater Dallas Community of Churches. Together they wrote a column for the *Dallas Morning News* that asked people to make the effort to get beyond the quick—but often incorrect—answers provided by prejudice based on stereotypes (simple and inaccurate images of the members of a particular racial or ethnic group).

Things to remember while reading "Blaming Bombing on Muslims Shows Prevalence of Prejudice":

- The Oklahoma City bombing happened during the eight-month-long trial of Egyptian Muslim sheikh (an Arab village or clan leader) Omar Abdul Rahman and nine other Arabs for planning numerous terrorist attacks in New York City. A year earlier, four of the sheikh's followers had been convicted for the dramatic 1993 bombing of the 110-story World Trade Center, which killed six people and injured one thousand others.

- For seventeen days after the Oklahoma City bombing, rescuers searched through the ruins of the building, trying to find survivors or remains of victims. These efforts received a great deal of media attention.

- Although 90 percent of early Middle Eastern immigrants were Christians, many recent arrivals have been Muslims; today, half of Arab Americans are Muslims. Only 20 percent of the world's Muslims are Arabs; in America only 12 percent of Muslims are Arabs. Nevertheless, many people think that Muslims and Arabs are the same, possibly because the pictures they have seen of Muslims praying in mosques (places of worship) show people wearing Arab-style clothing.

"Blaming Bombing on Muslims Shows Prevalence of Prejudice"

Less than a week after the bombing of the Alfred P. Murrah Federal Building in Oklahoma City, leaders of the Muslim and Christian communities of the Dallas [Texas] area met to listen and respond to each other's experiences during those terrible days.

Our group of thirty persons representing two mosques and a number of Christian congregations has been meeting regularly for about eighteen months, gradually becoming acquainted with each other as persons and growing in our understanding of our respective faith traditions and cultures. Our Muslim-Christian Dialogue Group was **convened** by the Muslim Community of North Texas and the Greater Dallas Community of Churches.

We knew each other well enough that the Muslim members were willing to share something of the hurt which they felt immediately after the bombing. Within twenty minutes of the first announcement that "Middle Eastern men" had been seen outside of the federal building, the Dallas mosques began to receive threats. Hateful messages were left on the Islamic Association's answering machine. Someone threw a bag into the child-care center operated by a mosque and hollered "Bomb!"

There was a quick and thoughtful response by the Muslim community. Instead of rightful anger, they went to work. A blood drive was organized the day after the bombing. A collection in all of the mosques was held, and a check was delivered to Oklahoma City officials. Later, a delegation traveled to Oklahoma City to help with a children's center and a feeding center and to participate in the memorial service.

When it became fairly clear that the bombing was not the work of "Middle Eastern terrorists," several unknown persons called or came to the mosque to apologize for having jumped to hurtful conclusions.

Our group decided to share our thoughts about these events with members of our respective communities. We also share them with our fellow citizens through this column.

It is time for public **reaffirmation** that we have all been created by the one God, that we are members of one human family and that we seek to live with one another in peace and to treat one another justly.

We all need to remember that we are a nation of many peoples. Together we are the unique cultural mosaic that is the United States of America. Through our diversity we strengthen and enrich one another.

In the aftermath of this great tragedy that has touched all our lives and hearts, we need to recognize and deal with the prejudice

Convened: Assembled.

Reaffirmation: Remindful statement.

which **permeates** our culture. It was reflected in some of the media reports which from the beginning—and even after emerging evidence pointed in other directions—made references to "Middle-Eastern men" and "Islamic **terrorism.**" Those reports created a climate of fear and hysteria regarding recent immigrants, especially those from the Middle East and persons of the Muslim faith, making them an easy **scapegoat** when a villain was needed.

Islam is a religion which seeks peace, as does Christianity and all other genuine world religions. Religious names should not be used to describe terrorism. The word "terrorism" is too often used exclusively with respect to actions by persons or groups from other nations, while it is seldom used to refer to groups or individuals in our own nation who use force.

The media, government officials and all of us as citizens need to make a commitment to be slow in placing blame. Had our law enforcement agencies not been able to work as quickly as they did in this case, we fear that mosques all over the nation would have been vandalized and that persons who looked "Middle Eastern" would have been harassed in a frenzy of hatred.

If this tragedy has taught us anything, it is that we must come together in a spirit of love and support, without regard to national origin or religion. The rescue personnel and support groups from our own religious communities and elsewhere who traveled to Oklahoma City to offer their services to the wounded and **bereaved** set an example for all of us and demonstrated what can be achieved by good neighbors working together.

We are especially grateful for the large group of persons of the Islamic faith, many of Middle Eastern origin, who went from Dallas with willing hands and generous financial assistance for those in need. They helped us remember that in a time of tragedy like this, it is important to focus on the needs of the victims and their families.

We do regret that Muslim representatives were not included in the official memorial service in Oklahoma City, for whatever reason, and commend the citizens of Oklahoma City and Dallas who expressed their gratitude and apologies to the members of the Islamic community who offered their assistance to those in need. (Saleh and Quigley in Dallas Morning News)

Permeates: Saturates; is spread throughout.

Terrorism: The use of violence or threats to frighten or to intimidate a group or government into giving in to the terrorist's demands, usually political.

Scapegoat: Person to blame.

Bereaved: Deprived by death or by force.

American Perceptions of Arabs

"Americans hold generally negative views of Arabs and of specific Arab peoples, such as Palestinians, Lebanese, etc., although the general category of 'the Arabs' elicits more negative reactions than any of the countries or peoples constituting the Arab world," wrote Michael Suleiman in *Arab Americans: Continuity & Change* in 1989. Referring to a 1981 poll, Suleiman wrote that Americans saw Arabs as "simultaneously rich and 'backward, primitive, uncivilized,' people who dressed strangely, mistreated women, and appeared to be 'warlike, blood-thirsty,' 'treacherous, cunning,' 'strong, powerful,' and 'barbaric, cruel.'"

According to a six-day poll that happened to begin on the day of the Oklahoma City bombing, public perception of Arab Americans actually improved over the previous year:

- 48 percent of Americans believed there is a tendency to discriminate against Muslims in the United States; one year earlier, only 42 percent thought so.

- 45 percent believed that Muslims tend to be "religious fanatics" (unreasonable and extreme); 31 percent did not think so. One year earlier, only 24 percent did not think so.

- 37 percent believed that "Muslims tend to lead clean and respectable lives."

- 35 percent believed that "the vast majority of Muslims hate terrorism"; 25 percent did not think so.

A 1996 poll of American Muslims found that 41 percent thought they had suffered discrimination because of their religion; 58 percent did not feel they personally had experienced such treatment.

What happened next . . .

Muslim representatives were not invited to help conduct the nondenominational (not restricted to one religion or sect) memorial service honoring the victims of the explosion. However, several Muslim delegations from around the country attended the service. Across the nation, Muslim groups issued public statements condemning the bombing, organized blood drives to benefit the people injured in the blast, and collected money to help the victims and their families.

After the bombing, the Council on American-Islamic Relations (CAIR) surveyed Muslims in the United States

Media Responsibility

The Council on American-Islamic Relations (CAIR) studied the surge of hostility that confronted American Muslims after the Oklahoma City bombing. The published report of that study, *A Rush to Judgment: A Special Report on Anti-Muslim Stereotyping, Harassment and Hate Crimes following the Bombing of Oklahoma City's Murrah Federal Building, April 19, 1995,* included seventeen examples of biased or inflammatory statements that appeared on television, on radio, or in the newspapers within two days of the explosion. For example:

- One network television reporter said the scene "resembled Beirut," creating or reinforcing a link between the destruction and a terrorist event in the Middle East.

- A network television anchor interviewed a former police commissioner of New York City who compared the event to the bombing of the World Trade Center by Muslim extremists.

- An "expert" on terrorism (whose opinions are disputed by prominent American Muslims) said on national television, "This was done with the intent to inflict as many casualties as possible. That is a Middle Eastern trait."

- When sketches of two white suspects were made public, a national television reporter said, "There is still a possibility that there could have been some sort of connection to Middle East terrorism." He explained that an unnamed law-enforcement source had said the suspects had possibly been hired to rent the truck that was used in the bombing.

to find out how media coverage of the incident had affected them and released their findings in *A Rush to Judgment: A Special Report on Anti-Muslim Stereotyping, Harassment and Hate Crimes following the Bombing of Oklahoma City's Murrah Federal Building, April 19, 1995.* Half of those who responded to the survey said they were afraid for their children or the female members of their families (who dressed in a distinctively Muslim manner) to go out in public. One-fourth of those who responded thought that ignorance about the Muslim religion was "the main cause of anti-Muslim/Arab feelings." To try to solve this problem, CAIR published booklets explaining Islamic religious practices to employers and to teachers.

Did you know . . .

- In 1990, the American-Arab Anti-Discrimination Committee (ADC) received reports of 39 incidents in which Arab Americans were harassed; the following year, it received 119 reports (according to *The Detroit News*). CAIR, which has been monitoring harassment of American Muslims since the Oklahoma City bombing, received reports of 280 episodes of bias or stereotyping in 1997; of those, 36 involved actual harassment or violence, compared with 85 in 1996 (when a residence building housing U.S. soldiers was bombed in Saudi Arabia, killing 19 and seriously injuring hundreds).

- American citizens, businesses, and government installations are the target of one-third of all terrorist incidents around the world. Most of those incidents happen outside the United States.

- In 1997, thirteen internationally related terrorist incidents happened in the United States. Twelve were letter bombs mailed from Egypt, and one was a random shooting in which a Palestinian man killed one person and injured several others in New York City.

For More Information

Abu-Laban, Baha, and Michael W. Suleiman, eds. *Arab Americans: Continuity & Change.* Belmont, MA: Association of Arab-American University Graduates, 1989.

"Attitudes towards Moslems Improve." *Middle East Mirror,* May 4, 1995. Available at http://www.iap.org/news/MSANews/199505/19950517.0. html (April 1999).

Saleh, Ghassan, and Tom Quigley. "Blaming Bombing on Muslims Shows Prevalence of Prejudice." *Dallas Morning News,* May 13, 1995, p. 4G. Reprinted in *A Rush to Judgment: A Special Report on Anti-Muslim Stereotyping, Harassment and Hate Crimes following the Bombing of Oklahoma City's Murrah Federal Building, April 19, 1995.* Washington, DC: Council on American-Islamic Relations, 1995.

Shepardson, David. "Mood: Local Arabs Fear Attacks, Bias." *The Detroit News,* February 8, 1998. Available at http://detnews.com/1998/metro/9802/08/02080088.htm (October 20, 1999).

"Study Shows Marked Increase in Reports of Anti-Muslim Discrimination." Press release from the Council on American-Islamic Relations (CAIR), July 15, 1998. Available in the News Releases (1998) section of http://www.cair-net.org (October 20, 1999).

Magdoline Asfahani

"Time to Look and Listen: Thanksgiving Reminds Us That Our Differences Unite Us and Make Us Unique as a Nation"
Newsweek article
Published December 2, 1996

A terrible civil war raged in Lebanon from 1975 until 1991. During just the first two years of that war, 60,000 Lebanese people were killed. In the United States, television news broadcasts frequently showed the ruins of bombed buildings in downtown Beirut, the capital of Lebanon. From 1978 until 1984, military forces from the United States and other countries belonging to the United Nations (UN), a worldwide organization devoted to keeping peace among nations, tried unsuccessfully to end the war in Lebanon. The UN troops withdrew after terrorist attacks against them on October 23, 1983, killed more than 300 people. Finally, in 1991, the rival Christian and Muslim factions agreed on a compromise government that guarantees each group a powerful role.

Magdoline Asfahani (c. 1973–), a Syrian-Lebanese American, grew up during this sixteen-year period, when Lebanon was nothing more than a symbol of violence and destruction to most Americans. In 1996, while she was studying political science at the University of Texas at El Paso, Asfahani saw *Executive Decision,* one of many films about Arab or Muslim terrorists attacking the United States. She decided it was time to

"Suddenly, those years of watching movies that mocked me and listening to others who knew nothing about Arabs and Muslims except what they saw on television seemed like a bad dream. I knew then that I would never be silent again."

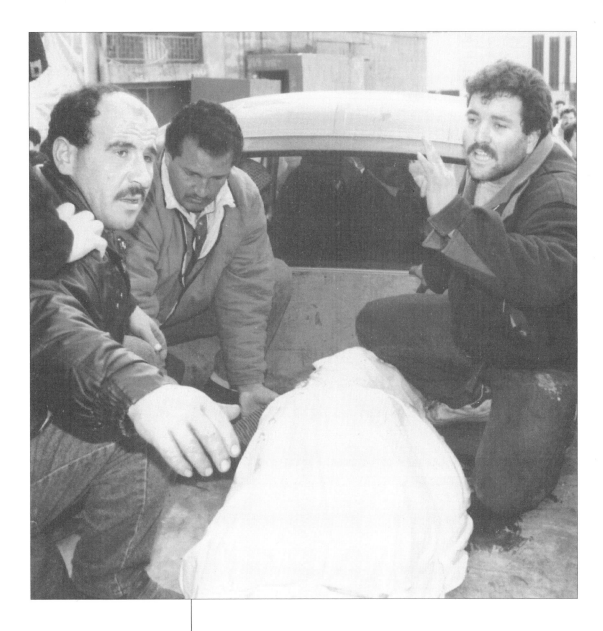

Arab American Voices

Palestinians surround the body of a Palestinian killed by a Jewish settler in 1994. The Middle East has been a symbol of violence and destruction since the 1940s. *Reproduced by permission of Corbis–Reuters.*

share her thoughts and experiences with a national audience, so she wrote an essay and sent it to *Newsweek* magazine.

Things to remember while reading "Time to Look and Listen":

- On June 14, 1985, two Lebanese Muslim extremists hijacked (took control of) TWA Flight 847 after it took off from Athens, Greece. The airplane was supposed to go to Rome, Italy, but the hijackers forced the pilot to fly to Beirut. They held control of the plane for seventeen days, forcing the pilot to fly between Beirut and Algeria four times. They killed one passenger but eventually released the other 152 passengers and crew members. The hijackers escaped, but one of them was arrested in Germany in 1987. In 1989, he was convicted of murder and hijacking and was sentenced to life in prison.

- In April 1983, a car containing a bomb exploded at the U.S. embassy (government building) in Beirut, killing 63 people. Six months later, another bomb exploded at a U.S. Marine barracks (residence building) in Beirut, killing 241 people.

- On April 19, 1995, a bomb hidden in a truck parked in front of a federal office building in Oklahoma City, Oklahoma, exploded. It destroyed the building, killing 168 people and injuring 600 others. At first, the police suspected that Arab terrorists were responsible, but the two men who were finally convicted of the crime were white Americans with no Arab connections.

"Time to Look and Listen"

*I love my country as many who have been here for generations cannot. Perhaps that's because I'm the child of immigrants, raised with a **conscious** respect for America that many people take for granted. My parents chose this country because it offered them a new life, freedom and possibilities. But I learned at a young age that the country we loved so much did not feel the same way about us.*

*Discrimination is not unique to America. It occurs in any country that allows immigration. Anyone who is unlike the majority is looked at a little suspiciously, dealt with a little differently. The fact that I wasn't part of the majority never occurred to me. I knew that I was an Arab and a Muslim. This meant nothing to me. At school I stood up to say the Pledge of Allegiance every day. These things did not seem **incompatible** at all. Then everything changed for me, sudden-*

Conscious: Thoughtful; deliberate.

Incompatible: Opposite to each other; incapable of blending together.

ly and permanently, in 1985. I was only in seventh grade, but that was the beginning of my political education.

That year a TWA plane originating in Athens was **diverted** to Beirut. Two years earlier the U.S. Marine barracks in Beirut had been bombed. That seemed to start a chain of events that would forever link Arabs with **terrorism.** After the hijacking, I faced classmates who taunted me with cruel names, attacking my heritage and my religion. I became an outcast and had to apologize for myself constantly.

After a while, I tried to forget my heritage. No matter what race, religion or ethnicity, a child who is attacked often retreats. I was the only Arab I knew of in my class, so I had no one in my **peer group** as an ally. No matter what my parents tried to tell me about my proud cultural history, I would ignore it. My classmates told me I came from an uncivilized, brutal place, that Arabs were by nature anti-American, and I believed them. They did not know the hours my parents spent studying, working, trying to preserve part of their old lives while embracing, willingly, the new.

I tried to forget the Arabic I knew, because if I didn't I'd be forever linked to murderers. I stopped inviting friends over for dinner, because I thought the food we ate was "weird." I lied about where my parents had come from. Their accents (although they spoke English perfectly) humiliated me. Though Islam is a major **monotheistic** religion with many similarities to Judaism and Christianity, there were no holidays near Chanukah or Christmas, nothing to tie me to the "Judeo-Christian" tradition. I felt more excluded. I slowly began to turn into someone without a past.

Civil war was raging in Lebanon, and all that Americans saw of that country was destruction and violence. Every other movie seemed to feature Arab terrorists. The most common questions I was asked were if I had ever ridden a camel or if my family lived in tents. I felt burdened with responsibility. Why should an **adolescent** be asked questions like "Is it true you hate Jews and you want Israel destroyed?" I didn't hate anybody. My parents had never said anything even **alluding to** such **sentiments.** I was confused and hurt.

As I grew older and began to form my own opinions, my embarrassment lessened and my anger grew. The turning point came in high school. My grandmother had become very ill, and it was necessary for me to leave school a few days before Christmas vacation. My chemistry teacher was very sympathetic until I said I was going to the Middle East. "Don't come back in a **body bag**" he said cheer-

Diverted: Forced to change course.

Terrorism: The use of violence or threats to frighten or to intimidate a group or government into giving into the terrorist's demands, usually political.

Peer group: Group of friends and classmates.

Monotheistic: Believing that there is only one God.

Adolescent: Teenager.

Alluding to: Hinting at.

Sentiments: Thoughts; beliefs.

Body bag: A bag in which corpses are placed.

fully. The class laughed. Suddenly, those years of watching movies that mocked me and listening to others who knew nothing about Arabs and Muslims except what they saw on television seemed like a bad dream. I knew then that I would never be silent again.

I've tried to **reclaim** those lost years. I realize now that I come from a culture that has a rich history. The Arab world is a medley of people of different religions; not every Arab is a Muslim, and vice versa. The Arabs brought tremendous advances in the sciences and mathematics, as well as creating a literary tradition that has never been surpassed. The language itself is flexible and beautiful, with **nuances** and shades of meaning unparalleled in any language. Though many find it hard to believe, Islam has made progress in women's rights. There is a specific provision in the **Koran** that permits women to own property and ensures that their inheritance is protected—although recent events have shown that interpretation of these laws can vary.

My youngest brother, who is twelve, is now at the crossroads I faced. When initial reports of the Oklahoma City bombing pointed to "Arab-looking individuals" as the culprits, he came home from school crying, "Mom, why do Muslims kill people? Why are the Arabs so bad?" She was angry and brokenhearted, but tried to handle the situation in the best way possible: through education. She went to his class, armed with Arabic music, pictures, traditional dress and cookies. She brought a chapter of the social-studies book to life, and the children asked intelligent, thoughtful questions, even after the class was over. Some even asked if she was coming back. When my brother came home, he was excited and proud instead of ashamed.

I only recently told my mother about my past experience. Maybe if I had told her then, I would have been better equipped to deal with the thoughtless teasing. But, fortunately, the world is changing. Although discrimination and **stereotyping** still exist, many people are trying to lessen and end it. Teachers, schools and the media are showing greater sensitivity to cultural issues. However, there is still much that needs to be done, not for the sake of any particular ethnic or cultural group but for the sake of our country.

The America that I love is one that values freedom and the differences of its people. Education is the key to understanding. As Americans we need to take a little time to look and listen carefully to what is around us and not rush to judgment without knowing all the facts. And we must never be ashamed of our pasts. It is our collec-

Reclaim: Recover; take back.

Nuances: Hints.

Koran: The Muslim holy book.

Stereotyping: Holding a simple and inaccurate image of the members of a particular racial or ethnic group.

tive differences that unite us and make us unique as a nation. It's what determines our present and our future. (Asfahani in Newsweek*)*

What happened next . . .

After Asfahani's article appeared in *Newsweek,* she received mail from many readers. "I was surprised by how many people said they cried when they read my article," she told the editor of the *Cafe Arabica* Internet Web site. "I didn't expect it to move them so deeply—and not only Arabs. . . . In fact, a Hispanic mother told me she was also affected by it because it reminded her of her own experiences as an immigrant."

Did you know . . .

• During the eighth and ninth centuries, Baghdad (now the capital of Iraq) became a center of learning, where scholars gathered to translate and study scientific and mathematical books from other cultures. Muhammed ibn Musa al-Khwarizmi (783–850), an Arab mathematician, developed the decimal place-value number system that is still used throughout the world. He also invented algebra, a method of solving problems using equations.

• Iraqi scientist Abu Ali Hasan Ibn al-Haitham (965–1040) has been called the father of modern optics, the study of light and vision. He conducted experiments and developed theories about such topics as shadows, rainbows, and the physical nature of light.

• Thabit Ibn Qurrah (836–901) was an Arab scientist who wrote books on mathematics, astronomy (the study of the universe), and medicine. His analysis of how forces balance objects at rest laid the foundation for the modern study of statics. The techniques he developed for figuring out the surface area and volume of solid objects were early versions of the modern mathematical field of integral calculus.

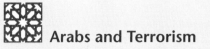

Arabs and Terrorism

Terrorism, according to United States law, means "premeditated, politically motivated violence' perpetrated against noncombatant targets by subnational groups or clandestine agents, usually intended to influence an audience." That is, terrorist acts are violent actions that are planned in advance and that target civilians and unarmed or off-duty members of the military. They are not official acts of any government, but they may be secretly supported by a government. Terrorists act to draw attention to their political goals and to try to force opposing governments to meet their demands.

Magdoline Asfahani described the 1983 bombing of a Marine barracks in Beirut as the start of "a chain of events that would forever link Arabs with terrorism." Indeed, radical Arab or Muslim individuals or groups staged at least a dozen spectacular airplane hijackings and bombings against American government facilities and citizens over the next fifteen years. However, there were also many terrorist episodes in other parts of the world during that period—places like Ireland, India (often involving non-Arab Muslims), and Colombia, South America (often directed at U.S. citizens or American businesses).

In its annual report *Patterns of Global Terrorism,* the U.S. Department of State reported that 40 percent of the international terrorist events in 1998 were aimed at U.S. targets. Three-fourths of those took place in Colombia and had nothing to do with Arabs or Muslims. On the other hand, all twelve of the U.S. citizens killed in terrorist attacks in 1998 died in a bomb attack in Africa that was planned by Usama Bin Ladin, a Saudi Arabian whose citizenship has been canceled because of his terrorist activities. The report listed 118 "significant terrorist events" of 1998; U.S. citizens or American-owned companies were involved in only 18. Fewer than half of those (eight) were committed by Arabs or Muslims.

For More Information

Asfahani, Magdoline. "Time to Look and Listen: Thanksgiving Reminds Us That Our Differences Unite Us and Make Us Unique as a Nation." *Newsweek,* December 2, 1996, p. 18.

"History of Islamic Science." *Islamic Alchemy in the Context of Islamic Science.* Available at http://www.levity.com/alchemy/islam.html (May 1999).

"*Newsweek* Article by Arab American Student Recounts Pain of Stereotyping." *Cafe Arabica* Culture Section. Available at http://www.cafearabica.com/culture/cultmagdoline7x2.html (February 1999).

Patterns of Global Terrorism: 1998. U.S. Department of State. Available at http://www.state.gov/www/global/terrorism (May 1999).

Zana Macki

"Take a Lesson from History and End Arab-American Discrimination before It's Too Late"

Detroit News guest editorial
Published October 14, 1998

I n 1995 the United States experienced the worst terrorist attack in its history when a bomb destroyed a federal office
building in Oklahoma City, Oklahoma, killing 168 people and
injuring 600 others. (A terrorist act is a violent or threatening
act, such as a bombing, used to force a group or government
to give in to the terrorist's demands, usually political.) The following year, in an effort to give the government more effective ways of preventing terrorism, Congress passed the Antiterrorism and Effective Death Penalty Act (AEDPA). Although
preventing terrorism is a good objective, many people are concerned that this law and the way it has been applied violate
basic elements of the American system of government.

One of the most controversial aspects of AEDPA is
that it allows the government to arrest people for certain
types of crimes based on secret evidence. Specifically, the government can arrest and even deport (force to leave the country) aliens (non-U.S. citizens living in the United States) without having to show them—or their lawyers—the evidence
that the government has collected showing that the person
was intending to commit a terrorist act. Similarly, anyone can

"The evidence against
them is so secret, that
even the defendant's
lawyers are not allowed
to see, review, and
challenge it in any way,
shape or form. All this
under the guise of
national security."

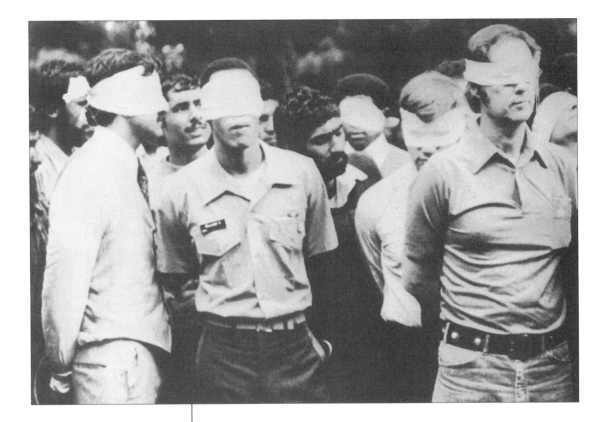

American hostages taken from the U.S. Embassy in Tehran, Iran, by militant students, November 4, 1979. The Iran Hostage Crisis contributed to negative feelings toward Arabs in the United States. *Reproduced by permission of UPI/Corbis–Bettmann.*

be prosecuted for donating money, work, or goods to an organization the government has labeled a "foreign terrorist organization"; again, the government does not have to provide them with the evidence. Without knowing why the government suspects them of such activity, these people cannot disprove the charges or explain their actions.

The Fifth and Sixth Amendments to the U.S. Constitution guarantee every person the right to proper legal procedures and the right "to be informed of the nature and cause of the accusation [and] to be confronted with the witnesses against him." Such constitutional protections normally apply not only to citizens but also to noncitizens while they are in the United States. Some secret-evidence portions of AEDPA apply only to noncitizens; others apply to citizens as well.

The *New York Times* reported in August 1998 that at that time secret evidence was being used against twenty-five persons, all of whom were either Muslims or were of Arab ancestry. Zana Macki, an executive in various Arab American organizations, including the American-Arab Anti-Discrimination Committee (ADC) and the Muslim American Alliance (MAA), discussed her concerns about the secret-evidence aspect of AEDPA as well as discrimination against Arab Americans in general in a column published in the *Detroit News*. Macki was concerned not only about discrimination against her ethnic and religious group, but also about the possibility that all Americans could lose some fundamental rights if the law were applied to other ethnic, religious, or political groups.

Things to remember while reading "Take a Lesson from History and End Arab-American Discrimination before It's Too Late":

- On December 21, 1988, Pan Am Flight 103 exploded over Lockerbie, Scotland, killing 270 people, 189 of them Americans. Three years later, investigators identified two men whom they believed placed a suitcase containing a bomb on the plane. The men were intelligence officers in Libya, an Arab country in northern Africa. Libya's dictator, Muammar al-Qaddafi (1942–), actively supported terrorism in many parts of the world, and he refused to turn the suspects over to the American or British governments for prosecution. In 1999, after seven years of economic and political pressure on Libya, the United Nations persuaded Gadhafi to send the men to the Netherlands for trial under Scottish law.

- The 1980 Iranian crisis Macki mentions involved a hostage situation that lasted more than a year. On November 4, 1979, a group of students seized the U.S. Embassy in Tehran, the capital of Iran. The terrorists were upset because the American government was helping the former ruler of Iran, who was overthrown earlier that year and whom they wanted to put on trial. They took sixty-six Americans hostage. Five months later, the United States attempted a surprise attack to rescue the hostages, but the plan failed when two American helicopters collided and crashed. The militants finally agreed to release the hostages on January 20, 1981.

- On June 14, 1985, two Muslim extremists from Lebanon hijacked TWA Flight 847 after it took off from Athens, Greece. The flight was supposed to go to Rome, Italy, but the hijackers forced the pilot to fly to Beirut, Lebanon. They controlled the plane for seventeen days and killed one passenger. The other 152 passengers and crew were finally released, and the hijackers escaped. One was arrested in Germany in January 1987. In May 1989, he was convicted of murder and hijacking and was sentenced to life in prison.

- The Persian Gulf War took place between January 17 and February 28, 1991. Iraq had invaded Kuwait to take over its valuable oil resources. United Nations forces, a large portion of which were American, drove the Iraqi forces out of Kuwait.

"Take a Lesson from History and End Arab-American Discrimination before It's Too Late"

One of my African-American friends actually encouraged me to tell people I was Hispanic. "Come on Zana! You have dark hair, brown eyes, and olive skin. You look more Mexican than Arab."

I was stunned. Why would I pose as being something that I was not? Another woman lectured, "Well, you better tell your people they can't bomb us. You tell them we're Americans and they won't get away with it."

*These comments were made shortly after the bombing of Pan Am Flight 103. Sometimes I think some people actually believe Muslims are born with a **terrorist** gene. Over the years, the anti-Arab/Muslim sentiment has grown tremendously.*

*The Detroit area is the home of the largest Arab-American population outside the Middle East, with approximately 250,000 people. I remember during the 1970s, there were very few of us. I was born here, and was not a queer "**boater**."*

*More and more Arabs began arriving into the United States to escape oppressive **regimes** or simply to (seek after) the American dream. In 1980, during the **Iranian crisis**, I was attending school at*

Terrorist: A person who uses violence or threats to frighten or intimidate a group or government into giving in to the terrorist's demands, usually political.

Boater: An immigrant who arrived by ship.

Regimes: Governments.

Iranian crisis: The Iran Hostage Crisis began on November 4, 1979, when a group of Iranian students seized the U.S. Embassy in Tehran, the capital of Iran, and took sixty-six Americans hostage, holding them for fourteen months.

Michigan State University. One Iranian girl screamed from her balcony as kids threw her bicycle over the balcony and chanted, "Foreign go home."

My roommates began treating me differently. They started mocking Iranians as crazy Arabs. They did not even realize Iranians are not Arabs, but even if they were, does it make sense to **scapegoat** whole groups of people?

Even my cousin Jamal shaved off his mustache because people thought he was Iranian. My cousin Eddie's camel oil jacket went into the closet and a hushed silence swept the community.

Once a cable show labeled me as: Lebanese-Arab-Shiite woman. That would be like labeling someone as Irish-American-Protestant man.

There was even a U.S.-backed plan to round up Arab **nationals** and put them in so-called detention camps in Texas shortly after the bombing of TWA Flight 847. In reality, they would have been modern day **concentration camps**.

During the Persian Gulf War, I was working for the American-Arab Anti-Discrimination Committee. One retired army general called and said, "Bang, bang, you're dead." A kid called in and said you have ten minutes before a bomb goes off.

One of my **covered** aunts was accused at the mall, and the community went inward. One talk radio host gave a new meaning to the phrase "talk is cheap." He started calling Arabs "rag-heads," and [saying] they believe in becoming **martyrs**. Let's show them a quick way to **Allah**.

Let us not forget the way Japanese-Americans were treated during **Pearl Harbor**. Japanese-Americans were uprooted from their homes, stripped of their self-worth, and placed into so-called internment camps. We vowed never, never again.

Yet hundreds of Arab immigrants from around the country are being picked up by the Immigration and Naturalization Service for **visa** violations. Many are immediately turned over to the FBI [Federal Bureau of Investigation] on the basis of being a suspected terrorist.

The evidence against them is so secret, that even the defendant's lawyers are not allowed to see, review, and challenge it in any way, shape or form. All this under the guise of national security.

Scapegoat: Blame.

Nationals: People belonging to a nation.

Concentration camps: Camps where war prisoners, political prisoners, or refugees are confined.

Covered: Wearing the traditional Muslim clothing that fully covers the arms, legs, and head.

Martyrs: People who die for a just cause.

Allah: God.

Pearl Harbor: A U.S. Navy base in Hawaii that was attacked by Japan in 1941, drawing the United States into World War II.

Visa: Official permission to enter a country.

*On the contrary, the use of secret evidence is national insecurity. Let's not throw out the Constitution, including appropriate checks and balances. The United States is a free and open society, not a closed **KGB**-style dictatorship. Whatever the alleged crime, everyone is entitled to a fair and democratic trial. Everyone.*

It is frightening to realize that whole groups of people, in particular Muslims, are treated as worse as the Japanese. During times of international crisis, we are openly scapegoated.

*Some of our **mosques** have been burned, our lives threatened, and we have been harassed at work, at school and by our neighbors. We have become **open season** on the air-waves with many journalists equating Muslims with terrorists without distinction.*

Our mosques, schools, businesses and neighborhoods must be protected. So must our basic constitutional rights. For if they are not, who is to say what group is next? (Macki in Detroit News*)*

What happened next . . .

In a lawsuit that was decided in late 1995, before AEDPA became law, several judges ruled that the government could not use secret evidence in its efforts to deport two Palestinian Arabs. "This is a great decision," said David Cole, one of the Palestinians' lawyers. "It confirms that the government has to play fair against everyone, aliens and citizens alike." He added that the decision implied that the secret-evidence portion of AEDPA, which Congress was considering at that time, would be unconstitutional.

The first lawsuit challenging AEDPA to reach the U.S. Supreme Court was decided in 1999. In its review of lower court decisions, the Supreme Court chose not to consider the question of secret evidence, but only whether the government could target certain groups for deportation. The case involved the same two Palestinian refugees, along with five other Arabs. The Supreme Court agreed to hear arguments about whether immigrants facing deportation could appeal to

KGB: The secret police agency that investigated citizens who disagreed with the government of the Union of Soviet Socialist Republics (Soviet Union).

Mosques: Muslim places of worship.

Open season: Targets of criticism; refers to the period that hunting is allowed in certain areas.

Zana Macki Fights Prejudice

Lebanese American Zana Macki has been active in Arab American organizations since about 1990. After working in the Detroit, Michigan, office of the American-Arab Anti-Discrimination Committee (ADC), she became the regional coordinator for that national group. She served as the executive director of the Muslim American Alliance (MAA). One of her missions is to battle stereotypes, simple and inaccurate images of the members of a particular racial or ethnic group, by increasing Americans' understanding of Muslims.

Macki stresses the diversity of the Muslim community. Like Christians and Jews, Muslims may be fundamentalists who insist on a strict, literal interpretation of their scriptures, or they may be liberals who focus more on the general ideas behind their beliefs than on specific rules, or they may interpret their religious beliefs in a moderate way that lies between the two. She points out that if a Christian extremist shoots an abortion doctor, that does not mean all Christians are murderous fanatics;

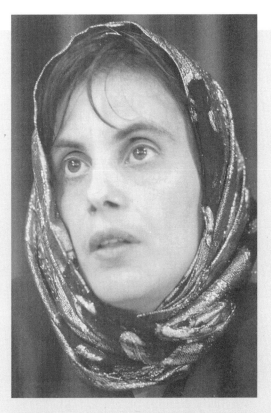

Zana Macki. *Reproduced by permission of AP/Wide World Photos.*

if a Jewish American is arrested for stealing government secrets, it does not mean all Jews are spies; and if a Muslim radical bombs an office building, it does not mean all Muslims are terrorists.

federal district courts if they thought they were not getting justice in the immigration courts. It decided they could not.

In the same decision, the Supreme Court also ruled that the president and the Justice Department "should not have to disclose its 'real' reasons for deeming nationals of a particular country a special threat—or indeed for simply wish-

How Good Is the Secret Evidence?

"Evidence deemed so sensitive it is kept secret while being used to jail or deport dozens of U.S. residents as terrorists has proved, when revealed, to be flimsy and bigoted," an October 1998 article in the *St. Petersburg Times* revealed. In a few cases, those who had been accused or their attorneys finally obtained formerly secret evidence. Here are some examples the article described:

- Imad Hamad, a Palestinian refugee living in Michigan since 1980, was charged with belonging to a terrorist organization. After an immigration judge ruled in 1997 that Hamad could stay in the United States with his wife and children, Hamad received most of the evidence the government had used. It stated that the Federal Bureau of Investigation (FBI) had stopped investigating him in 1990 after finding "no information . . . which would justify continued investigation of Hamad, as investigation failed to prove Hamad's

activities on behalf of the [suspect organization] were terrorist in nature."

- The government tried to deport six Iraqi refugees based on "evidence" such as this:

  One of the defendants, a doctor in the Iraqi military, "told agents he did not cut off the ears of deserters, a purported Iraqi punishment. FBI agents said [he] worked in a military hospital, so he must have cut off ears."

  One of the defendants, who had guarded Scud missiles while he was in the Iraqi military during the Persian Gulf War, said he had not seen a missile launch. "The FBI said he must have and is lying."

  An FBI agent wrote, "I didn't like [one defendant's] whole demeanor [way of carrying himself] when I was talking to him. . . . It's been my experience working with these people that they lie, they lie an awful lot."

ing to antagonize a particular foreign country by focusing on that country's nationals." In other words, immigration officials could target certain ethnic groups for deportation hearings. "We were blindsided," said Cole. Upset by the surprise extension of the ruling beyond what the court had agreed to decide, Cole said they issued the ruling "after telling us not to address that issue." He had not been allowed to present reasons why the government should not be able to selectively target certain groups. With the support of numerous civil rights organizations, the American-Arab Anti-Discrimination Committee (ADC) asked the Supreme Court to rehear the case.

Did you know . . .

• "The word 'Allah' is interpreted as a 'different' God than the God of Christians and Jews, when in fact it is just another word for the same God, such as 'Yahweh' and 'Jehovah,'" wrote Palestinian American author Ray Hanania. "All Arabs, be they Christian or Muslim, use the term Allah to refer to God."

• During World War II (1939–45), Japan was one of the United States' main enemies. Fearing that Japanese Americans would help Japan invade America, the U.S. government moved more than 100,000 people of Japanese ancestry to internment camps, where they lived until the end of the war. They had to leave their homes and businesses, which they lost. The camps were closed after the war ended. In 1988 Congress formally apologized and paid $20,000 to each victim who was still alive.

For More Information

"ADC Stunned by Supreme Court Attack on Immigrants' Rights." *American-Arab Anti-Discrimination Committee.* Available at http://www.adc.org/press/press.html (April 1999).

Aschoff, Susan. "At Last Unveiled, Evidence Falls Short." *St. Petersburg Times* (Florida), October 4, 1998. Available at http://www.sptimes.com/Worldandnation/100498/At_last_unveiled_evi.html (October 20, 1999.)

"Federal Judge Rules Government Cannot Use Secret Evidence in Long-Running Deportation Case against Palestinians." American Civil Liberties Union (ACLU) press release. Available at http://www.aclu.org/news/n012495.html (May 1999).

Hanania, Ray. "Hollywood Must Be More Responsible." *Arab Media Syndicate,* October 22, 1998. Available in the Columns section of http://www.hanania.com (May 1999).

Macki, Zana. "Take a Lesson from History and End Arab-American Discrimination before It's Too Late." *Detroit News,* October 14, 1998.

Rubin, Neal. "Arab Way Has Tough Defender: Zana Macki Chips Away at Abundant Stereotypes." *Dallas Morning News,* February 3, 1999, p. 4C.

Smothers, Ronald. "U.S. Bars or Expels Suspect Immigrants on Secret Evidence." *New York Times,* August 15, 1998, p. A1.

Atif Harden

"The American Muslim Council:
There Need Not to Be a 'Clash of Civilizations'
between Islam and the U.S."
**Excerpt from congressional testimony submitted to the National
Security, International Affairs and Criminal Justice Sub-Committee
of the House Government Reform and Oversight Committee
Delivered October 2, 1998**

The best known Hebrew [Jewish-language] word in American culture is *shalom,* meaning *peace.* The best known Arabic word is *jihad,*" Georgetown University Professor Yvonne Haddad told a reporter in 1998. The American press typically translates *jihad* as "holy war," using it to describe terrorist activities of Muslim extremists who want to destroy non-Muslim societies, such as the United States. (A terrorist act is a violent or threatening act, such as a bombing, used to force a group or government to give in to the terrorist's demands, usually political.) Like many stereotypes, that translation of *jihad* goes unquestioned by people who accept what they hear or read, especially when it is short and simple. However, most Muslims interpret *jihad* as "struggle." "In our private lives we make a jihad—a struggle—to lead our lives in a manner consistent with the code of ethics embodied in the Quran," or Koran, the Muslim holy book, wrote Atif Harden, executive director of the American Muslim Council, in "An Islamic Perspective on Civic Participation." Harden explained that the Koran challenges Muslims to "struggle for peace and the principles of our faith: justice, love, charity, patience, honesty, and truth."

"The American Muslim population and its organizations pose no violent threat to the United States and our way of life. Speaking as an American, I am weary of hearing and seeing Islam and Muslims portrayed as foreign and different. We are cousins of Jews and Christians. We worship the same God, follow the teachings of the same prophets, and believe in the same books."

A group of Muslim demonstrators bow in prayer at a peaceful demonstration outside the White House in Washington, D.C., December 1987. Though there are a handful of Muslims who are terrorists, the vast majority of Muslims try to live their lives in accordance with the laws of the Koran.
Reproduced by permission of AP/Wide World Photos.

Misunderstandings like the real meaning of *jihad* contribute to inaccurate stereotypes of Arabs and Muslims. (Stereotypes are simple and inaccurate images of the members of a particular racial or ethnic group.) The August 1998 bombings of American embassies in the African nations of Kenya and Tanzania by followers of exiled Saudi Arabian terrorist Usama bin Laden reinforced the notion that Arabs and Muslims are the most dangerous terrorist threat to the United States. Concerned that actions being considered by Congress would focus unfairly on these ethnic and religious groups, Harden decided to offer lawkmakers his insights and suggestions as an official spokesman for American Muslims. In a statement to a U.S. House of Representatives committee in October 1998, he tried to correct some of those misunderstandings, especially with respect to terrorism.

Because of some dramatic incidents of terrorism by people who justify their violence in the name of the Muslim religion, a stereotype has arisen linking Muslims, Arabs, and terrorism. In fact, Muslims (people whose religion is Islam) and Arabs (people whose ancestral language is Arabic) are not the same group: in the United States and around the world, most Muslims are non-Arab, and only about one-half of Arab Americans are Muslims. And very few Muslims or Arabs are terrorists. "Islam by definition derives meaning from the word *peace*," Harden also wrote in his statement on civic participation. The *Islam Voice* Web site explains that "The word *Islam* has a two-fold meaning: peace, and submission to God. . . . Once we humble ourselves, rid ourselves of our egoism and submit totally to Allah [God] . . . we will surely feel peace in our hearts."

Things to remember while reading "The American Muslim Council: There Need Not to Be a 'Clash of Civilizations' between Islam and the U.S.":

- During the 1950s, there was great tension between the United States and the communist Union of Soviet Socialist Republics (Soviet Union). The basic idea of communism is that each person contributes a fair share of work to society, and in return each person receives the things he or she needs, like food, shelter, and medical care. However, communism in the Soviet Union was a brutal form of government in which its citizens were little more than slaves of the state. Some Americans joined the Communist political party because they believed in the basic idea of communism. Senator Joseph R. McCarthy (1908–1957) conducted hearings that got a great deal of media attention, charging that people who belonged to the Communist Party wanted to help the Soviet Union destroy the United States. Many people lost their jobs because he accused them of being Communists, but he never proved that any of them wanted to harm the U.S. government.

- In more than forty-five countries, Islam is the largest religion. Followers of Islam are called Muslims. Some of the Muslim nations, like Egypt, Syria, and Saudi Arabia, are Arab countries. However, the six largest Muslim nations—Indonesia, Bangladesh, Nigeria, Pakistan, Turkey, and Iran—are not Arab countries.

- Timothy McVeigh, an American terrorist, blew up a federal office building in Oklahoma City, Oklahoma, in 1995, killing 168 people and injuring 600 others. He was angry with the U.S. government for killing 81 members of a religious cult in a confrontation outside Waco, Texas, two years earlier.

- There was a great deal of political conflict in the United States during the 1960s and 1970s, primarily involving civil rights activists seeking equal treatment for African Americans and antiwar protesters opposing the Vietnam War (1965–75, when U.S. forces tried to keep communist North Vietnam from taking over noncommunist South Vietnam). Although nonviolent civil rights activist Martin Luther King Jr. (1929–1968) spoke at its organizing meeting, the Student Nonviolent Coordinating Committee (SNCC, pronounced "snick") gradually became a militant organization and dropped the word *nonviolent* from its name, changing it to the Student National Coordinating Committee. The Students for a Democratic Society (SDS) also began as a civil rights group, but it shifted its focus to opposing the Vietnam War. SDS also became increasingly militant; some of its members formed the Weathermen, an organization that tried to bring about an American revolution through terrorist bombings.

McCarthy: (1908–1957) Joseph R. McCarthy was a U.S. senator who led a national anticommunist movement during the 1950s.

Unethical: Unprincipled; dishonest.

Asserting: Strongly claiming.

Muslims: People whose religion is Islam.

Terrorism: The use of violence or threats to frighten or to intimidate a group or government into giving in to the terrorist's demands, usually political.

"The American Muslim Council: There Need Not to Be a 'Clash of Civilizations' between Islam and the U.S."

*Good morning Mr. Chairman and other distinguished members of the committee. I come before you today to pronounce that there need not to be a "clash of civilizations" between Islam and the United States. Further, you should reject the **McCarthy**-like tactic, used by some **unethical** people, of **asserting** that Islam, **Muslims** and American Muslim organizations endorse **terrorism**. You are here* today to discuss solutions to the problem of terrorism. The American Muslim community shares your concern regarding this plague. As the Executive Director of the American Muslim Council I would like to propose a measure that may help remedy the problem.

But first I would like to talk about the American Muslim community and the recent **bigotry** that we have had to endure concerning this question of terrorism. Mr. Chairman the American Muslim population and its organizations pose no violent threat to the United States and our way of life. Speaking as an American, I am weary of hearing and seeing Islam and Muslims portrayed as foreign and different. We are cousins of Jews and Christians. We worship the same God, follow the teachings of the same prophets, and believe in the same books. We are all followers of **Abraham.** Islam is not new to our homeland. There is strong evidence that Muslims were trading with the Americas before Columbus "discovered" the New World. Many more Muslims came in the holds of slave ships. We literally helped build this nation. Our roots are deep in America, and as immigrants from the Middle East, North Africa, the **sub-continent,** Southeast Asia, and the Balkans arrive, they continue to enrich us.

Mr. Chairman I can proudly say to you today that the Muslim community in America is the model minority community in the United States. We are a value driven community that shares a faith that is pro-family, pro-education, anti-racist, pro-business, law abiding, and anti-crime. There are no Arab, Pakistani, Somalian, Senegalese or Indonesian ghettos in the United States. Muslims living in disadvantaged communities are often the lights of those communities, promoting family, education, cleanliness, **chastity, self-sufficiency,** and zero tolerance towards drugs and the mental slavery that **blight** produces. We are one of the best-educated groups in the nation, and have one of the lowest crime rates. Because of our commitment to serve God and our country Muslim doctors, lawyers, teachers, accountants, and businessmen are serving in inner city and rural communities that no one else in the country is attracted to.

Mr. Chairman, let me answer some questions for you and the committee. Is terrorism a **tenet** of Islam? No!

Are Muslims, or those who claim Islam as their motive, sometimes involved in terrorist acts? Yes.

Are Muslims involved in the majority or at least in a significant number of domestic terrorist attacks? According to the FBI [Federal Bureau of Investigation], no!

Bigotry: Prejudice; discrimination.

Abraham: An early prophet, or holy man.

Subcontinent: India, Bangladesh, Bhutan, Nepal Pakistan, and Sikkim, countries located on a large peninsula in southeast Asia.

Chastity: Abstaining from having sexual relations outside of marriage.

Self-sufficiency: The quality of relying upon oneself, not on others.

Blight: Something that frustrates or destroys.

Tenet: Central belief.

Doctrine: Religious teachings.

Credence: Credit; acceptance as truth.

Stereotyping: Holding a simple and inaccurate image of the members of a particular racial or ethnic group.

Pope: The leader of the Catholic Church.

Mafia: A criminal organization, many members of which are Italian.

Fifth column: People in one country who are secretly working for an enemy country.

Unfounded: Not based on fact.

Patently: Obviously.

Interning: Confining to camps, as prisoners of war.

Legitimacy: Legality; righteousness.

Radicals: People who hold beliefs different from those of most other people.

Marginalized: Placed on the outer edge of acceptability or society.

Inadequate: Inferior.

Grievances: Complaints.

Is the killing of innocent men, women and children supportable by Islamic religious **doctrine?** *No! . . .*

Mr. Chairman, given our long history, commitment and contribution to our nation, I hope that in our public policy statements concerning Islam and Muslims, we don't repeat the mistakes of the past. You must resist those who want to blame and demonize an entire community for the crimes of a few. Let us not give **credence** *to the bigotry of those who will say that "Islam is a terrorist religion" or "all Muslims are terrorists" or "American Muslim organizations are front groups for terrorists." We already know the danger and stupidity of mass* **stereotyping.** *Mr. Chairman, we didn't elect a Catholic president until this century, because people feared that a Catholic would be under the control of the* **Pope.** *Others believe that we can't have an Italian president because he would be under the influence of the* **Mafia.** *And still others believe that Jews are a* **fifth column** *that can't be trusted and whose loyalty will never lie with the United States. All of these fears have not only proven to be* **unfounded,** *but it is* **patently** *ridiculous to stereotype entire groups in this manner. Mr. Chairman, we let our fears get out of control in the past, and we made a terrible mistake with the Japanese American community by* **interning** *them during the Second World War [1939–45]. Our national shame and regret over this incident continues to haunt us.*

Let's not make this same mistake with Islam and the Muslim community. . . .

It is important that we realize that the significance or **legitimacy** *of a cause is not diminished because of the actions of a few* **radicals.** *Every significant movement in this country has been plagued by radical excess. The Independence Movement, the Anti-slavery Movement, the Labor Movement, the Civil Rights Movement, the Anti-war Movement, the Environmentalist Movement, the Animal Rights Movement, and now even the Anti-abortion Movement. Terrorist acts occur when groups or individuals feel ignored,* **marginalized** *and* **inadequate** *facing a superior force. People's [terrorist] tactics must be condemned, but their legitimate* **grievances** *must still be addressed.*

Mr. Chairman I would now like to recommend a policy position. I would like to suggest that in order for us to effectively fight this problem of terrorism that we look closely not only at the effects of this horrible problem, but also at its causes.

Therefore, Mr. Chairman, I would like to recommend that the President and/or Congress establish a National Commission on the Causes and Prevention of Terrorism. I know that Congress has proposed a committee on counter-terrorism, but that will only deal with the effects of the problem. . . .

*Imagine how many lives would have been saved if **Timothy McVeigh** could have told us what was troubling him and those like him. It is easy for people to condemn him and his like for the awful crime they committed, but we have to still ask ourselves why his complaints and grievances couldn't have been addressed through our political system. Granted, some people are just criminal, but what harm would it do us to establish dialogue with political **dissidents?** . . . Please look for a moment at how we dealt with radical anti-war groups **(SDS)** and the radical civil rights groups **(SNCC)** in the 70's. First we took the route of demonizing them, but that only played into their hands and **empowered** them. But then we started to dialogue with them and began to address some of their core concerns, like poverty, homelessness and the **de-escalation** of war in **Vietnam**. With their problems being addressed and solutions formulated, it took away their anger and frustration. Now, in fact, many of them are respected contributing members of the establishment that they once **abhorred**.*

*Mr. Chairman, we will not be able to solve all of the problems posed by the **right and left wing groups** that employ terrorist tactics, but we can dialogue with them and present to them a system that is not **intransigent**, one-sided, and is at least perceived to be fair. (Harden, "American Muslim Council")*

What happened next . . .

On September 9, 1998, three weeks before Harden submitted his testimony to Congress, Representative Frank Wolf introduced a bill that would create a National Commission on Terrorism. After the House of Representatives and the Senate approved the concept, President Bill Clinton signed it into law

Timothy McVeigh: The American terrorist who was found guilty of bombing the federal office building in Oklahoma City, Oklahoma, in 1995, killing 168 people and injuring 600 others.

Dissidents: People who oppose the government, church, or some other authoritative organization.

(SDS): Students for a Democratic Society.

(SNCC): Student Nonviolent Coordinating Committee.

Empowered: Make more confident; strengthen.

De-escalation: Decreasing the intensity.

Vietnam: Southeast Asian country where the United States fought an unpopular war from about 1965 to 1975.

Abhorred: Hated.

Right and left wing groups: In general, groups that want to maintain traditional values (right wing or conservative) versus groups that want change (left wing or progressive).

Intransigent: Refusing to agree or compromise.

The U.S. Government's Counterterrorism Policy

In his congressional testimony, Atif Harden commented that the government's current counterterrorism policies deal only with effects, not causes, of terrorism. In fact, the only prevention strategies mentioned in official statements of American policy deal with limiting terrorists' access to weapons and money and discovering plans for terrorist attacks. The following statements are two examples.

In February 1999, U.S. Attorney General Janet Reno told a Senate committee:

> The Federal Bureau of Investigation (FBI) is the lead agency for responding to acts of domestic terrorism [terrorism on U.S. soil]. The FBI continues to work to identify, prevent, deter, and defeat terrorist operations before they occur. We will not always be able to prevent every incident and we will have to respond to terrorist incidents here and abroad. In these instances the FBI will lead the federal response to a domestic terrorist incident through the coordinated crisis response mechanism of its

Counter-Terrorism Section. . . . The National Infrastructure Protection Center (NIPC) in the FBI is now a reality and is working to detect and respond to cyber-based [computer network] attacks on our critical infrastructures.

In April 1999, U.S. Secretary of State Madeleine Albright made public the annual report *Patterns of Global Terrorism.* In an accompanying statement, she wrote:

> We do all we can to put pressure on terrorists all the time, not just when they are about to strike. In cooperation with other governments, we go after terrorist finances, shut down illegal activities, restrict travel, disrupt training, break up support cells [groups] and bring suspects to justice.
>
> In our efforts, we use a wide range of foreign policy tools, from military force when necessary, to vigorous diplomacy, the negotiation of treaties, the enforcement of laws, the sharing of information, the offering of rewards, the development of new technology and the improvement of our security.

on October 21, 1998. The ten experts Congress appointed to the commission were expected to review current government policies on terrorism and to recommend improvements. Several Arab American groups were concerned, however, that the commission would be biased against Arabs and Muslims. In fact, an October 19, 1998, editorial in the *Minnesota Daily* said:

> We are questioning the balance and objectivity of the proposed commission because of Wolf's legislative history, his apparent focus on Islam and Muslims and from a statement that

Rep. Wolf attached to his bill. The statement focuses specifically on "Middle-Eastern terrorism" [without naming any other area] and recommends several people to be on the commission who clearly have anti-Arab and anti-Muslim biases.

For example, one of the people Wolf recommended for the commission had written in a 1990 magazine article, "Western European societies are unprepared for the massive immigration of brown-skinned peoples cooking strange foods and maintaining different standards of hygiene."

Did you know . . .

- During the sixteenth, seventeenth, and eighteenth centuries, more than ten million Africans were brought to America as slaves. According to the Islamic Information Office, more than 30 percent of them were Muslims.

- Muslims believe the Koran contains God's messages to his prophet Muhammad (c. 570–632), just as the Torah (Jewish scripture) and the Christian gospel contain God's messages to his prophets Moses and Jesus.

- Some historians believe Muslims sailed between Africa and North America as early as 889. When Italian explorer Christopher Columbus (1451–1506) "discovered" America in 1492, he found, among other evidence of earlier visits, a mosque (Muslim house of worship) and spears with tips made of a combination of metals exactly like those used by African Muslims.

- John F. Kennedy (1917–1963) was the first Catholic to be elected president of the United States. He took office in January 1961 and was assassinated less than three years later. Lee Harvey Oswald, an emotionally disturbed man who had lived in the Soviet Union for three years, was arrested for shooting Kennedy, but he was murdered before he could be tried for the crime.

For More Information

Albright, Madeleine K. "Statement on Release of 'Patterns of Global Terrorism 1998' Report." Press release by the U.S. Department of State. Available at http://secretary.state.gov/www/statements/1999/990430.html (October 20, 1999).

"American Muslim History." Available on the Islamic Information Office Web site at http://iio.org/history/history.htm (May 1999).

"Editorial: Commission Biased Toward Arabs, Muslims." *Minnesota Daily,* October 19, 1998. Available at http://www.daily.umn.edu/daily/1998/10/19/editorial_opinions/oo19 (October 20, 1999).

Harden, Atif. "The American Muslim Council: There Need Not to Be a 'Clash of Civilizations' between Islam and the U.S." Testimony submitted to the National Security, International Affairs and Criminal Justice Sub-Committee of the House Government Reform and Oversight Committee (October 2, 1998). Available at http://www.arab-media.com/98octnovamc.html (February 1999).

Harden, Atif. "An Islamic Perspective on Civic Participation." *The Interfaith Alliance.* Available at http://www.tialliance.org/tia/press/pcbah.html (May 1999).

"Questions about Islam." Available on the *Islam Voice* Web site at http://www.islamvoice.com (May 1999).

Reno, Janet. "Statement of Janet Reno, Attorney General of the United States, before the United States Senate Committee on Appropriations Subcommittee on Commerce, Justice, and State, the Judiciary, and Related Agencies, February 4, 1999." Available at http://www.senate.gov/~appropriations/commerce/2499jr.htm (October 20, 1999).

Van Sertima, Ivan. *They Came before Columbus.* New York: Vintage Books, 1989.

Born in America

People who move to the United States from another country must adapt to a different culture. They have to decide which of their native customs to maintain in their families and which language to speak in their homes. They miss relatives and friends from their old country, even if they are happy with their decision to immigrate. They may face prejudice and discrimination because of their different appearance, accented English, or unfamiliarity with American customs.

Children or grandchildren of immigrants grow up knowing the American culture and language, but they face other challenges. Like **H. S. "Sam" Hamod**, they may be embarrassed by the strange accents and customs of their parents or grandparents. They may go through a period of confusion, not feeling fully American, yet not completely identifying with or being accepted in their ancestral culture. Eventually, most find a comfortable balance between their two cultures. Some become actively involved in their ethnic heritage; **James Abourezk**, for example, worked on Middle East peace efforts while he was a U.S. senator and devoted his efforts to Arab American issues after that.

In 1992 Barbara C. Aswad, then the president of the Middle East Studies Association, spoke about the conflicts faced by descendants of immigrants. She began with the following observations:

> As I contemplated today's topic, I was thinking of my many experiences while teaching in the heart of Arab communities in Detroit, where a mini-skirted, second generation Iraqi Chaldean [a member of the Chaldean Christian religion] sits next to an African-American Muslim fully covered except for her eyes. Or an Iraqi Christian boy, majoring in social work, who falls in love with the Yemeni Muslim girl sitting next to him. She is among the first women of that community to enter college. Their parents break up the romance causing the young people much suffering, and the Iraqi youth is sent to Iraq, a country he has never seen, to become engaged to his cousin. After he returns to the U.S., the Gulf War erupts and he, being a U.S. marine who speaks Iraqi Arabic, is sent to Saudi Arabia under a Polish name to guard Iraqi prisoners of war. Meanwhile, America executes one of the largest bombing raids in history on his ancestral home, in which his new fiancee waits for a visa [permission to enter the United States].
>
> The conflicts and multilayered identity crises are great for this young Arab American of twenty years. But he explains that equally difficult is his father's insistence that he take over the family grocery store while he wants to become a social worker, an occupation scorned by his father. The 50,000 Iraqis in his [Michigan] community had anguished over the fate of their relatives, and feared for their own safety, as flags and ribbons blanketed the neighborhoods. Most suffered in painful silence, afraid to speak. After the war, relief efforts united them with local Arab groups, both Christian and Muslim, such as the Lebanese and Palestinians, who had suffered in the past and with whom they had barely interacted previously. Of course the recent Detroit headlines which read "Kuwait Tank Deal Saves Michigan Jobs" (*Detroit Free Press* October 13, 1992) is also a fundamental part of the equation. [That is, an emotional conflict arises from the fact that Iraqi immigrants earn a living building tanks that may be used in a war against Iraq.]

For More Information

Aswad, Barbara C. "Arab Americans: Those Who Followed Columbus." *Middle East Studies Association Bulletin,* July 1993. Available at http://w3fp.arizona.edu/mesassoc/Bulletin/aswad.htm (October 20, 1999).

James Abourezk

"Remarks to AAUG Annual Convention"

**Excerpts from the keynote address of the
Arab-American University Graduate annual convention
Delivered October 19, 1996**

J ames Abourezk was born in 1931 in South Dakota and has lived in the United States all his life, but his Arab heritage is an important part of his life. He grew up on a Sioux reservation where the only non-Indians were himself, his parents (who had immigrated from Lebanon), his four brothers and sisters, and another Arab family. Before he started elementary school, Abourezk spoke only Arabic.

Abourezk (pronounced AB-oor-ezk) was seventeen years old in 1948 when Israel was established as a Jewish nation in the Middle East, on land that had belonged to Palestinian Arabs. During World War II (1939–45), Adolf Hitler, leader of Germany, and his Nazi Party followers murdered six million Jews and after the war most of the world supported establishing a homeland where Jews could feel safe. The main opposition to Israel came from Arabs whose land was given to the Jews, and from neighboring Arab countries that considered the Jews to be outsiders who forced their way into the area. Since that time there has been constant tension and frequent violence between Israel and its Arab neighbors.

"Over the years we, as Arab Americans, have been unable to come to complete terms with who we are, and what we are, and I believe the blame rests for the most part on the Arab–Israeli conflict, and its fallout."

149

James Abourezk. *Reproduced by permission of Corbis Corporation (Bellevue).*

Like most Americans, Abourezk felt sympathy for the new Jewish nation. "For most of my adult life I had believed that Israel had been picked on by the Arab countries," Abourezk wrote in his autobiography, *Advise and Dissent: Memoirs of South Dakota and the U.S. Senate*. But in 1973, a year after he was elected to the United States Senate, Abourezk visited Beirut, Lebanon, where he got what he called the "shock of [his] life." Seeing Arab families living in flimsy shacks beside open sewers and children playing in piles of rubble created by Israeli bombs made him more sympathetic to the Arab side in the continuing Middle East conflict. Abourezk chose not to run for reelection to the Senate, and in 1980 he founded the American-Arab Anti-Discrimination Committee (ADC) to reunite Arab Americans and to raise their self-image. He was still serving as an adviser to the ADC when he was invited to deliver the keynote address (main speech) at the annual convention of the Association of Arab-American University Graduates (AAUG) in Anaheim, California in 1996.

Things to remember while reading "Remarks to AAUG Annual Convention":

- In 1973 the Arab countries of Egypt and Syria attacked Israel to recapture land Israel had taken from them in the Six Day War of 1967. Because the United States helped Israel during the 1973 war, the oil-producing Arab nations refused to sell oil to United States customers. Americans became worried that they would not be able to operate their cars and heat their homes; people had to wait in long lines at gas stations, and prices rose. However, Abourezk wrote in his autobiography, "We were then importing no more than 6 percent of our oil from the Arab oil exporting countries. But making Arabs—all Arabs—the scapegoat for our economic problems was too convenient for demagogic [gaining power by raising people's prejudices] politicians, multinational oil companies, and, of course the Israeli lobby" (a group of people who try to persuade government leaders to support their cause).

- Yasir Arafat (1929–) was elected president of Palestine in 1989, even though it did not exist as a physical country. In 1993 Arafat and Israel's prime minister, Yitzhak Rabin (1922–1995), reached a peace agreement in which Israel promised to withdraw from the Arab lands it had captured in the 1967 war. Arafat's critics, including Abourezk, thought the agreement was weak, that Israel had no intention of returning the land to the Arabs so they could establish the nation of Palestine.

- Binyamin Netanyahu (also spelled Benjamin; 1949–) was elected prime minister of Israel in 1996. By destroying Arab homes and building new ones for Jewish settlers in the territories Israel had taken in 1967, Netanyahu demonstrated his unwillingness to give the land back to the Arabs. Netanyahu was turned out of office in 1999, defeated by Ehud Barak (1942–), who promised to resume peace talks with the Palestinians.

"Remarks to AAUG Annual Convention"

*My father died prematurely at the age of 79. But he had lived one great life, as short as it was. He immigrated to South Dakota in 1898, working for a time as a lawman, as a **homesteader**, and as a **pack-peddler** very much like the ancestors of people in this room. He finally settled on the Rosebud Sioux Indian reservation in South Dakota, eventually opening two general stores in two small towns near each other. . . .*

*My father had no identity crisis. I suppose that was because where he lived in America, and how he lived, didn't leave time for that kind of negative **introspection**. But neither was the **Palestin-***

Homesteader: An early settler who purchased land from the government at a low price in exchange for farming it.

Pack-peddler: A door-to-door salesman who carried merchandise in a backpack.

Introspection: Self-examination.

Palestinian–Israeli conflict: Also known as the Arab–Israeli conflict, hostilities between some Arab nations and Israel that began with the founding of the state of Israel on Palestinian Arab lands in 1948.

Havoc: Confusion, destruction.

Arab–Israeli conflict: Hostilities between some Arab nations and Israel that began with the founding of the state of Israel on Palestinian Arab lands in 1948.

Fallout: Negative results.

Embargo: Ban on trade.

Diverse: Varying; wide-ranging.

Divert: Shift.

Negligence: Carelessness.

Domestic: Having to do with a home or home country.

Lobby: A group that attempts to persuade government leaders to support their interests when passing laws and economic policies.

Editorial writers: Journalists who write columns offering opinions on news events rather than delivering straight news.

On a silver platter: When something is given to a person without that person having to make any effort.

Regimes: Governments.

Maronite: A Syrian branch of the Roman Catholic Church.

Phalangist: A militant Christian political party that opposed the Muslim groups during the Lebanese civil war.

ian–Israeli conflict an issue back then, a conflict which has created social and political **havoc** with our community.

It unfortunately has created another conflict within ourselves. I say this because over the years we, as Arab Americans, have been unable to come to complete terms with who we are, and what we are, and I believe the blame rests for the most part on the **Arab–Israeli conflict,** and its **fallout.** . . .

But I trace the beginning of our self-doubts with the American—and the Israeli—response to the Arab oil **embargo.** That was when the massive public relations attack on Arabs—and by extension, Arab Americans—came. The attack was so heavy, and so massive, that we as a community did not know how to respond. It came from such **diverse** sources as the oil companies, who wanted to blame someone for their own greed; from American politicians, who wanted to **divert** blame from their own **negligence** in not controlling **domestic** oil prices; from the Israeli **lobby** and its supporters, who saw the danger to them of Arab oil and Arab money; and from American **editorial writers,** who are traditionally lazy, and who saw an issue handed to them **on a silver platter.** There was also something extremely mean-spirited in all this. American journalists began behaving like children in a schoolyard. You know what I mean . . . when one child goes down in the fighting, everyone begins kicking him. And that's what the American press was doing. . . .

Then, in 1975, when the Lebanese civil war erupted, the divisions between Arab **regimes** became magnified in Lebanon, and they became real here in America. Although religion had very little to do with the Lebanese conflict, the **Maronite** church in America tried to make it so. It became a game of the **Phalangist** leadership in Lebanon to force people in this country to choose sides, resulting in a serious split in loyalties here, just as it resulted in a deadly split in Lebanon. The fact that the Phalangists were being supported by Israel made the divisions even more pronounced, and, in fact, deepened the crisis of identity being suffered by many in our community for the first time. Many of our community felt the need to continue to support the Palestinian cause, but withheld their support in part because of how the media began portraying Palestinians as **terrorists,** and in part because of the split **engendered** by the Phalangists. By this time, the media began labeling all Palestinians as terrorists. If you will recall the ugly editorial cartoons, the movie and television portrayals, among other things. . . .

*That split, and that identity crisis continued **unabated** for years. As a community, we began to change that in 1980, when the community put together ADC [American-Arab Anti-Discrimination Committee]. Its specific purpose was to try to re-unite the entire Arab American community, and it succeeded, up to a point. As a community, we had some tremendous obstacles to surmount. The head of the Maronite church forbade its members from joining ADC, primarily because we refused to support the Phalangist cause in Lebanon. There were many people jealous of the rapid growth of ADC, resulting in a good deal of undercutting of its mission. . . . There was more than one group formed because people could not bear the thought of not being the leader. Although we know that is a carry-over from the old country attitudes, it had some effect on us here.*

Additionally, we had a great many in our community who feared the loss of their business if they took part in any political movements. This created a great many internal conflicts, resolved only by many Arab Americans refusing to take part in community political activities. . . .

Terrorists: People who use violence or threats to frighten or to intimidate a group or government into giving in to the terrorists' demands, usually political.

Engendered: Caused.

Unabated: With no decrease in intensity.

Arab American Unity and Activism

Since they first began arriving in America in the 1890s, Arab immigrants had formed social organizations to enjoy and preserve their heritage and to provide assistance for fellow immigrants and for fellow Arabs who remained in the Middle East. These organizations were usually formed by ethnic subgroups of Arabs, like Syrians or Maronite Catholics. But it was not until 1967 that a broad-based organization formed to improve Arab Americans' group image and to strengthen their unity for political purposes. In response to the anti-Arab emotions brought about by the Six Day War, the Association of Arab-American University Graduates (AAUG) was founded. Its goals include distributing accurate scientific, cultural, and educational information about the Arab world; establishing mutual understanding and respect between Arabs and Americans; and developing cooperation among Arab Americans to serve their community.

American-Arab Anti-Discrimination Committee (ADC), which James Abourezk founded in 1980, was formed specifically to combat stereotypes that have humiliated Americans of Arab descent. The ADC is an international organization with seventy chapters around the United States. Its efforts include cultural, educational, political, and civil rights activities. Abdeen Jabara, who was ADC president from 1986 to 1990, wrote in *Arab Americans: Continuity & Change*, that "What Abourezk brought to Arab-American organizing efforts was a strategy of mass action by a mass membership to achieve credibility, access, acceptance, and impact."

The AAUG and ADC, along with several other national and regional organizations, help Arab Americans learn about their heritage and discuss their common problems. Through unified efforts, tens of thousands of Arab Americans can counteract the negative stereotypes that have crept into American society.

Yasir Arafat: (1929–) head of the Palestine Liberation Organization (PLO) since 1968 and president of the Palestinian government-in-exile since 1996.

Efficacy: Power.

*Our identity crisis has become, I'm sad to say, magnified by the signing of the agreement with Israel by **Yasir Arafat**. Amid the great desire for this conflict to come to an end came serious doubts about the **efficacy** of the agreement, especially when it came to any benefits for the Palestinian people as a whole. Our community was, and is, torn between a desire to get it all over with, and the recognition that in return for Yasir Arafat being crowned president of a non-existent Palestine, he gave it all away. It was as if using a* sports analogy, someone blew a whistle in the middle of a play, and everyone just stopped, without finishing the play. Our community hoped for the best, but feared the worst. Because Arafat left all the important issues—that is, important to the Palestinian people—for later, he is, to use another analogy, left at the altar with a small bouquet of flowers, but with no [loved one]. The issues of **Jerusalem**, of settlements, of nationhood, all were left for later. Later is now here, and **Netanyahu** is not so anxious to step up to the altar with Arafat.

This is not so much an identity crisis, as a crisis of the spirit. Do we revert to our former **persona** as resisters of Israeli objectives? Or do we play along, hoping for the best?

I think, that in search of our identities, that our **benchmark** [should] be our principles—those same principles that most of us have stood upon from the beginning. . . .

We must stand firm, and we must fight smart. And we must be able to know the difference between principle and opportunism. Only then will our own identities take shape. (Abourezk, "Remarks to AAUG," pp. 1-5)

What happened next . . .

During Netanyahu's three years as prime minister of Israel, the Arabs and Israelis moved further away from a peaceful solution to their land disputes. In 1999, however, Ehud Barak (1942–) was elected prime minister of Israel, defeating Netanyahu. Barak promised to work out a peace agreement with Arafat that would bring a lasting peace between Arabs and Jews. A *Newsday* article written just after the election reported that Arab American and Muslim leaders in New York were cautiously hopeful that Barak would work harder than Netanyahu had on peace talks with Arafat. *Newsday* quoted an ADC spokesman as saying, "It's impossible to tell what kind of leader he will be. But there are positive signs in the growing peace [movement]."

Jerusalem: The capital of Israel, which had been divided between Jordan and Israel until 1967, but which now Israel controls. Palestinians want Jerusalem to be the capital of Palestine, but the Israelis want to keep the city undivided.

Netanyahu: Binyamin Netanyahu (1949–), Israeli prime minister from 1996 to 1999.

Persona: Role.

Benchmark: Standard; a point of reference from which progress can be measured.

Did you know . . .

- Like Abourezk's father, most Arabs who came to America before 1925 worked as peddlers until they saved enough money to open a store. The peddlers carried their merchandise in suitcases or in backpacks weighing as much as two hundred pounds.

- The Lebanese civil war that began in 1975 lasted nearly fifteen years. American news reports featuring photographs of the bomb-devastated capital of Beirut contributed to the negative image of Arabs as violent and destructive. Arab Americans found themselves included in this stereotype.

- From 1948 until 1967, Jerusalem was divided into an Old City, which belonged to Jordan, and a New City, which was the capital of Israel. During the Six Day War, Israel also took control of the Old City, which it has held ever since. Control of Jerusalem is an important issue in the Arab–Israeli conflict; the Palestinians want Jerusalem to be the capital of the nation of Palestine, but the Israelis want to keep the city undivided.

For More Information

Abourezk, James. *Advise and Dissent: Memoirs of South Dakota and the U.S. Senate.* Chicago: Lawrency Hill Books, 1989.

Abourezk, James. "Remarks to AAUG Annual Convention." Keynote address to Arab-American University graduates annual convention, October 19, 1996. Available at http://www.cafearabica.com/issue2 nov96/organizations/keynotes.html (February 1999).

Jabara, Abdeen. "A Strategy for Political Effectiveness." *Arab Americans: Continuity & Change.* Edited by Baha Abu-Laban and Michael W. Suleiman. Belmont, MA: Association of Arab-American University Graduates, Inc., 1989, pp. 201–05.

Janison, Dan, and Mohamad Bazzi. "NY Jewish Leaders Back Barak; They See Election as Hopeful Sign." *Newsday,* May 18, 1999, p. A04.

H. S. "Sam" Hamod

"After the Funeral of Assam Hamady"
Published in 1970

"Dying with the Wrong Name"
Published in 1979

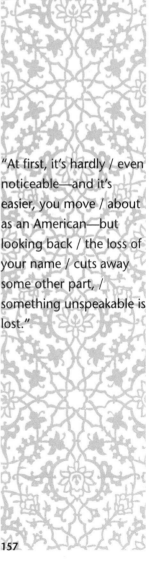

H amode Samuel "Sam" Hamod belongs to three cultures. By birth and citizenship, he is an American. Born in Indiana in 1936, he attended colleges in Illinois and Iowa. After earning a Ph.D. (a doctorate, the highest university degree), he taught English at several midwestern and eastern universities. He has also worked as a writer for two U.S. senators and two popular television comedy programs, *The Odd Couple* and *Happy Days*.

Ethnically, Hamod is an Arab whose father emigrated from Lebanon. The Arabic language is as important to his life as English is. Although it is not his primary occupation, Hamod has published eight books of verse. "I've always mixed Arabic with English in my poems," he told *Aramco World* magazine. "Certain things have more power in other languages." In *Grape Leaves,* an Arab American poetry collection that includes seven of his poems, Hamod wrote, "Our ethnicity helps shape the way we see and the way we write— so it is a part of what our poems are made of. But a poem cannot lean on its ethnicity in order to keep from falling—a poem must be a good poem on its own."

"At first, it's hardly / even noticeable—and it's easier, you move / about as an American—but looking back / the loss of your name / cuts away some other part, / something unspeakable is lost."

Religiously, Hamod is a Muslim whose father, an imam, built a mosque in Gary, Indiana. (An imam is a religious leader who conducts daily prayer sessions, gives sermons, and presides at weddings; a mosque is a Muslim house of worship.) Beginning in 1983, Hamod served for two years as director of the Islamic Center in Washington, D.C. Years earlier, the first director of the center had predicted that Hamod would someday hold that position. But Hamod thought that was unlikely for two reasons: he didn't consider himself a good enough Muslim, and he thought the international community would never choose an American to head the center, which is the focal point of the Islamic religion for North and South America. A humble man, Hamod was honored to direct the Islamic Center.

Things to remember while reading selections from Hamod's poems:

- One of the main teachings of Islam is that all Muslims who are physically and financially able to do so should make at least one pilgrimage (religious journey) to Mecca, the holy city of Islam. This pilgrimage is called a *hajj,* and anyone who has made the pilgrimage is given a title of respect: *Hajj* for a man and *Haja* for a woman.

- Muslims are expected to pray five times every day: at dawn, noon, afternoon, sunset, and night. These prayers consist of chanting certain words while performing specific movements such as bowing, kneeling, and touching the forehead to the floor. Before praying, Muslims remove their shoes and wash their hands, mouth, nostrils, face, arms, head, ears, neck, and feet. To keep themselves clean while praying, they may use a prayer rug or a suitable cloth.

- Ellis Island, New York, was one of the main entrance points for immigrants to the United States from 1892 to 1954. Approximately twenty million people were interviewed and given physical examinations as they entered the country. Immigration officers had to figure out how to spell unusual-sounding Arabic names; they sometimes misunderstood timid or confused immigrants and wrote down only part of their names. Whatever the officers

wrote down became the immigrants' legal names in the United States.

- Arab parents are known as the father (or mother) of their oldest son—or oldest daughter if they have no sons. For example, if a couple's oldest son is named Hamode, the father would be called "Abu Hamode" and the mother would be called "Im'a Hamode."

Pilgrims at Mecca, the holy city of Islam. One of the main teachings of Islam is that all Muslims who are physically and financially able to do so should make at least one pilgrimage to Mecca. *Reproduced by permission of Corbis–Bettmann.*

"After the Funeral of Assam Hamady"
(For my mother, David and Laura)

Cast:
Hajj Abbass Habhab: my grandfather

Sine Hussin: an old friend of my father
Hussein Hamod Subh: my Father
me

6 p.m.

middle of South Dakota
after a funeral in Sioux Falls
my father and grandfather
ministered the Muslim burial
of their old friend, Assam Hamady

me—driving the 1950 Lincoln
ninety miles an hour

"STOP! STOP!
stop this car!"

Why?
"STOP THIS CAR RIGHT NOW!"—Hajj Abbass
                    grabbing my arm from the back seat
"Hysht Iyat?   (What're you yelling about?)"—my Father
"Shu bikkee?" (What's happening?)—Sine Hussin

I stop

"It's time to pray"—the Hajj
                yanks his Navajo blanket
                opening the door

"It's time to pray, **sullee**
the sun sets
time for sullee*"*

my Father and Sine Hussin follow
obedient
I'm sitting behind the wheel
watching, my motor still running

car lights scream by
more than I've ever seen in South Dakota

the Hajj spreads the blanket
blessing it as a prayer rug
they discuss which direction is **East**

after a few minutes it's decided
it must be that way
they face what must surely be South

Sullee: To pray.

East: Muslims should face
toward Mecca, in the east,
when praying.

they face their East, then notice
I'm not with them

"Hamode! get over here, to pray!"

No, I'll watch
and stand guard

"Guard from what—get over here!"
I get out of the car
but don't go to the blanket

My father says to the others:
"He's foolish, he doesn't know how
to pray."

they rub their hands
then rub their faces
rub their hands then
down their bodies
as if in **ablution**

their feet bare
together now
they begin singing
Three old men
chanting the **Qur'an** *in the middle*
of a South Dakota night

> **Allahu Ahkbar**
> Allahu Ahkbar
>
> Ash haduu n lah illah illilawhh
> Ash haduu n lah illah illilawhh
>
> Muhammed rasoul illawh

in high strained voices they chant

> Bismee lahee
> a rah'manee raheem

more cars flash by

> malik a youm a deen
> ehde nuseerota el mustakeem
> seyrota la theena

I'm embarrassed to be with them

Ablution: Ritual washing.

Qur'an: Also spelled Koran;
the Muslim holy book.

Allahu Ahkbar: God is the
greatest.

Immigrants arriving at Ellis Island, New York, in the early 1900s. Immigration officers had to figure out how to spell unusual-sounding names; whatever the officers wrote down became the immigrants' legal names in the United States. *Reproduced by permission of Corbis–Bettmann.*

Vigor: Energy.

en umta ailiy him
ghyrug mugthubee aliy him

people stream by, an old woman strains a gawk at them

willathouu leen—
Bismee lahee

I'm standing guard now

a rah'maneel raheem
khul hu wahu lahu uhud

*They're chanting with more **vigor** now
against the cars—washing away
in a dry state
Hamady's death
he floats from their mouths
wrapped in white*

Allahu sumud

lum yuulud wa'alum uulud

striped across his chest, with green

Walum yakun a kuf one uhud
willa thouu leen

his head in white, his grey mustache still

Ameen . . .

I hear them still singing
as I travel half-way across
America
to another job
burying my dead
I always liked trips, traveling at high speed
but they have surely passed me
as I am standing here now
trying so hard to join them
on that old prayer blanket—
*as if the pain behind my eyes could be **absolution***
(Hamod in Orfalea)

Dying with the Wrong Name
Three parts of an unfinished poem

(Dedicated to all the immigrants who lost their names at Ellis Island)

I.

These men died with the wrong names,
Na'aim Jazeeny, from the beautiful valley
of Jezzine, died as Nephew Sam,
Sine Hussin died without relatives and
because they cut away his last name
*at **Ellis Island**, there was no way to trace*
him back even to Lebanon, and Im'a Brahim
had no other name than mother of Brahim,
even my own father lost his, went from
Hussein Hamode Subh' to Sam Hamod.
There is something lost in the blood,
something lost down to the bone
in these small changes. A man in a
dark blue suit at Ellis Island says, with
tiredness and authority, "You only need two
names in America" and suddenly—as cleanly

Absolution: Forgiveness.

Ellis Island: In New York Harbor, a point of entry for immigrants to the United States.

Born in America: H. S. "Sam" Hamod | 163

as the air, you've lost
your name.   At first, it's hardly
even noticeable—and it's easier, you move
about as an American—but looking back
the loss of your name
cuts away some other part,
something unspeakable is lost. . . .

                                                                III

Even now, it's hard for me to
fully understand what this old **couple** *meant*
to my father—
his own father had died before my father came
to America in 1914, his mother still in Lebanon,
unseen for decades. My father is 39 or 40 now, I
am 4 or 5, we are constantly carrying groceries
to this old house, the old couple always says "no"
but then they take them, but only after we have
some **fatiyah** *and coffee, eat some fruit, talk*
(I'm usually impatient to go), then we climb back
into the car and go home. My father, a man I came to know
as so secretive, yet so generous, a man alone; now I know
this was part of that other reality, where his name, that
language, Hussein, Sine Hussin, Im'a Brahim, **Asalamu**
Aleikum,
all of these sounds were part of his name, this was that other
edge of Lebanon he carried with him, that home, that same
good food of the rich smells, it had to be in these moments,
these things
were not lost, but were alive and living in this room,
in this house, in these people, in this moment.
(Hamod in Orfalea, p. 169-72)

Couple: Sine Hussin and Im'a
Brahim.

Fatiyah: A bread pastry
stuffed with spinach and feta
cheese.

Asalamu Aleikum: Peace be
upon you (a common Muslim
greeting).

The Arabic Language

The Arabic language consists of two different versions. The written version, called Standard Arabic, is used throughout the Arab world. It was used to write the Koran—the first prose text written in Arabic—about 650 A.D. According to Muslim belief, the Koran contains God's revelations to the prophet Muhammad (c. 570–632). Because Muslims want to preserve the original meaning of the Koran, they have taken care not to change Standard Arabic since the seventh century. Most other languages have changed significantly over that period. For example, the works of English poet Geoffrey Chaucer (c. 1340–1400) are difficult for modern readers to understand, and even the English used by playwright and poet William Shakespeare (1564–1616) sounds strange to the modern ear.

Spoken Arabic, on the other hand, has many different forms. Dialects (regional variations in the language) may be so different that their speakers cannot understand one another. This is why some people talk about the "Lebanese language" and the "Egyptian language," for example, even though both are forms of Arabic.

Arabic consists of twenty-eight consonants and three vowels (each vowel has a long and a short sound). Written Arabic records only the consonants; based on the context, the reader figures out what vowels should be inserted in each word. For example, *h.s.b.* could mean *hasiba* (he thought), *hasaba* (he counted), *hasba* (according to), or *hasab* (of noble origin). Although a system has been developed for writing Arabic with the English alphabet, it is normally written in a script form that looks very different. Most letters have four different forms, depending on whether they are written alone or at the beginning, middle, or end of a word.

What happened next . . .

The American news media have begun to explore Islam for several reasons. For one thing, more than five million Muslims live in the United States in the 1990s, and Islam is the fastest-growing religion in the country. Also, there have been more than a dozen highly publicized terrorist attacks by Arab extremists calling themselves Muslims since 1983. Because of his expertise in the Muslim religion, the Arab culture, and the English language, Hamod thought he would be a logical source when reporters wanted information. Yet, even while he was director of the Islamic Center, his offers to talk to major television and radio networks were declined.

"They would have non-Muslims on the show talking about Islam or people with beards and heavy accents," Hamod wrote in *Konch* magazine. "There was no place for a Muslim who grew up and was educated in the U.S. My light skin and midwestern accent would have destroyed the stereotype that these media people were and are trying to perpetrate [carry out] against Islam. . . . I'll just go on being the best kind of Muslim and person that I can be, just trying to correct stereotypes against Muslims knowing full well that my voice and my face will rarely be heard or seen in the major media."

Did you know . . .

- In 1983, during Hamod's first year as director of the Islamic Center, a car containing a large bomb exploded at the U.S. embassy (government office building) in Beirut, Lebanon, killing sixty-three people. Six months later, another bomb exploded at a U.S. Marine barracks (residence building) in Beirut, killing 241 people. Over the next fifteen years, Arab terrorists committed at least a dozen spectacular airplane hijackings and bombings against American citizens or government facilities.

- "After the Funeral of Assam Hamady" was first published by the Perishable Press. The first edition consisted of 120 copies printed on handmade paper scented with thyme. The cover stock was made from flowers.

For More Information

Hamod, Sam. "Tyson, Muhammad Ali and Me." *Konch,* 1997. Available at http://www.ishmaelreedpub.com (May 1999).

"H.S. (Sam) Hamod." Orfalea, Gregory, and Sharif Elmusa, eds. *Grape Leaves: A Century of Arab American Poetry.* Salt Lake City: University of Utah Press, 1988, pp. 161–76.

Ruff, Carolyn. "Exploring Islam—The World's Second Biggest Religion also Is a Way of Life." *Washington Post,* May 13, 1998, p. H01. Available in the Articles section of http://www.playandlearn.org (October 20, 1999).

Simarski, Lynn Teo. "Poetry in the Blood." *Aramco World,* July/August 1990, pp. 50–54.

Women in
Arab American Communities

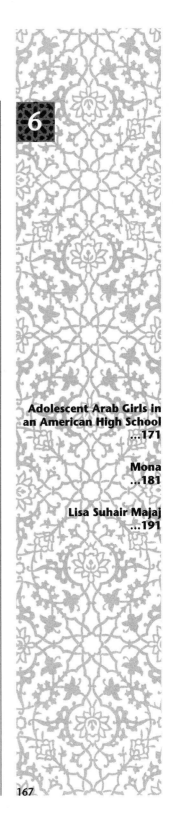

6

The two stereotypical images Americans have of Arab women are extreme opposites. One is of a quiet, passive woman who wears a heavy, flowing robe topped with a long scarf over her head, her face perhaps covered with a veil that reveals only her sad eyes. The other image is of a shimmying belly dancer in skimpy clothing, her bangles clinking in frantic rhythm with exotic music. Somewhere—in fact, everywhere—in between are real Arab women. In America, as in Arab countries, women have spirited discussions with their husbands, raise their children with the best values they can give them, work at tedious jobs and prestigious careers, and devote their energies to important political and social causes.

It is true that women hold a different place from men in Arab cultures. That place, rooted in the "different but equal" concept defined by Muslim scriptures, is theoretically a noble one. "In traditional Arab culture, the family is the center around which the sociomoral [social and moral] universe exists," Egyptian American anthropologist Fadwa El Guindi wrote in *Newsday*. "Women are the center of the family's sacred identity and the guardians of the Arab family's

Arab Muslim Women in History

Since the Islamic religion was founded in the seventh century, Arab women have fulfilled many roles, ranging from housewife to soldier. Some have risen to positions of prominence in politics, business, and entertainment. Here are a few examples:

The first woman to become a Muslim was the first wife of the prophet Muhammad (c. 570–632). Khadijah ul-Kubra' was a twice-widowed businesswoman who hired Muhammad and sent him on a business trip to Syria. He returned with twice the profit she expected. Their mutual admiration quickly developed into love, and she suggested marriage. She was forty years old, and he was twenty-five. They were devoted to each other throughout their forty-year marriage, which ended with her death. They had been married for fifteen years when a terrified Muhammad told her he had received a message from God through the angel Gabriel. She reassured and encouraged him then and during later revelations. Because she supported their family financially, Muhammad could spend his time preaching. Read more about Khadijah at http://www.geocities.com/Athens/Troy/1731/a_khadijah.html.

Sitt al-Mulk was a princess of the Muslim Fatimid empire, which ruled North Africa, Sicily, and Syria from Cairo (now in Egypt). In the year 996, her father died and her brother became caliph (ruler). Twenty-five years later, he disappeared, and she acted as ruler for forty days before arranging for her brother's son to be installed as caliph. She was named regent of the empire, acting as ruler on behalf of her young nephew. She was an effective and well-liked ruler until her death four years later. Find out more about her at http://www.amaan.com/current/sittul.htm.

Umm Kalthum's father was the imam (religious leader) of the mosque (Muslim house of worship) in a small village in northern Egypt. Even as a child, she had a remarkable singing voice; her father, who earned extra money by singing at weddings and other celebrations, helped her develop her talent. By 1920, when she was in her early teens, she was singing pro-

honor and reputation. Motherhood is considered sacred. Nationhood is expressed in 'motherland' terms. The Arabic words for women, household and sacred sanctity are close derivatives of the same root."

In practice, Arabs may fall short of the ideal, and limitations on women may overwhelm their theoretical (existing fessionally in concerts. She moved to Cairo in 1924 and quickly became the most popular singer in the Arab world. Umm Kalthum worked with composers and lyricists to create songs that flowed from the Egyptian and broader Arab cultures. A capable businesswoman, she also managed her own career. Her enormous popularity brought wealth, which she shared with the poor. During the 1950s and 1960s, she traveled throughout the Middle East as an unofficial ambassador, strengthening her country's relations with the leaders of other Arab nations. When she died in 1975, hundreds of thousands of fans walked behind the president of Egypt in a funeral procession more than a mile long. For more details about Umm Kalthum, see http://almashriq.hiof.no/egypt/700/780/umKoulthoum/biography.html.

Syrian American Lisa Halaby enrolled at Princeton University in New Jersey in 1970, the first year that prestigious college admitted female students. After graduation, she worked on urban-planning projects in the United States, Australia, Iran,

and Jordan. Later, she became the director of planning and design projects for the Royal Jordanian Airline. In 1978, after converting from Christianity to Islam, Halaby married Jordan's King Hussein (1935–1999) and became Queen Noor al-Hussein ("light of Hussein"). During the next twenty years, she was an active international advocate for such issues as women's rights and education. She served as president of the United World Colleges, which has ten multicultural campuses in countries around the world, and she chaired an advisory committee for the United Nations University International Leadership Academy. She founded the Noor Al Hussein Foundation to promote equal opportunity and self-reliance by helping welfare women develop their own businesses. Visit Queen Noor's Web site at http://www.noor.gov.jo/home.html

You can read about other prominent Islamic women in *Women in the Muslim World: Personalities and Perspectives from the Past* by Lyn Reese (Berkeley, CA: Women in World History Curriculum, 1998).

only in theory) position of honor. In restrictive Saudi Arabia, for example, women are not allowed to drive cars, and they must veil their faces in public. On the other hand, "In Syria, Arab school girls wear khaki uniforms and are required for school credit to work on urban improvement projects, planting trees and painting walls," Syrian American author Mona Fayad wrote in "The Arab Woman and I." She continued,

"Syrian television is constantly running ads for women to join the army."

In the United States, Arab American women are tremendously diverse. Roughly one-fourth of Arab Americans are Muslim women. The **Adolescent Arab Girls in an American High School** whom Charlene Eisenlohr interviewed faced the usual problems of American teenagers but with the added difficulty of cultural and religious standards that clash with those of mainstream America. **Mona**, a Palestinian American interviewed by Evelyn Shakir, struggled to develop her personal identity without violating her family's fundamental values. Christians, like **Lisa Suhair Majaj**, also face conflicts between their options as American women and their families' expectations based on Arab traditions.

For More Information

El Guindi, Fadwa. "UN Should Act to Protect Muslim Women." *Newsday*, April 13, 1998, p. A29.

Fayad, Mona. "The Arab Woman and I." *Food for Our Grandmothers: Writings by Arab-American and Arab-Canadian Feminists*. Edited by Joanna Kadi. Boston, MA: South End Press, 1994, pp. 170–72.

Adolescent Arab Girls in an American High School

"Adolescent Arab Girls in an American High School"
Selection from an interview conducted by Charlene Eisenlohr and published in *Family and Gender among Arab Americans*, edited by Barbara C. Aswad and Barbara Bilgé Published in 1996

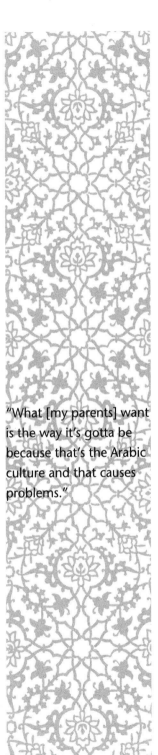

When Charlene Eisenlohr talked with Arab students in a Michigan high school, she found that they face two kinds of problems. Like all American teenagers, they struggle with their relationships with their parents and their siblings (brothers and sisters). They also face conflicts between mainstream American society and their ethnic culture.

Arab societies place different expectations on men and women. Women are viewed as the guardians of their family's honor and their community's reputation. They are expected to avoid any action or appearance that could bring dishonor. To help them avoid troublesome situations, their community restricts the type of clothing they can wear and activities they can take part in such as dating. Because their daughters' behavior reflects on the entire family's social standing, many Arab American parents are reluctant to relax these restrictions.

"What [my parents] want is the way it's gotta be because that's the Arabic culture and that causes problems."

Arab graduates at Fordson High School in Dearborn, Michigan, wear the traditional Muslim *hijab* beneath their mortar boards. Muslim women traditionally dress so as not to draw attention to themselves. *Reproduced by permission of Millard Berry.*

Things to remember while reading "Adolescent Arab Girls in an American High School":

- Dearborn, Michigan, has the largest Arab population outside the Middle East. At the high school where Eisenlohr conducted her interviews, 40 percent of the students had immigrated from Arab countries, especially Lebanon, Palestine, and Yemen. Many of the American-born students were also of Arab ancestry.

- Standards for appropriate clothing are generally based on rules of the Muslim religion, which originated in the Arab world. (Today, the population of most Arab countries is at least 90 percent Muslim; the exception is Lebanon, which is almost half Christian.) The basic requirement for both men and women is that they dress modestly. However, interpretations of the dress requirements for women vary. Some ethnic groups accept contemporary clothing as long as it covers the arms and legs and fits loosely. Some require a traditional ankle-length, shapeless dress with wrist-length sleeves.

- Because the family's honor depends on the behavior of its female members, some parents encourage (or even force) their daughters to marry someone of the parents' choice at an early age. However, such actions are culture-based rather than religion-based. The Koran (the Muslim holy book) says that a woman must not be forced into a marriage she does not want.

"Adolescent Arab Girls in an American High School"

[Charlene Eisenlohr asked the questions (labeled "Q:"). The names of the girls were changed to other, typical Arab names.]

THE GENERATION GAP

The conversation turned to some differences they had with their parents.

Q: How will you raise your children?

Inshad: Not the way I was raised. I would give them more freedom.

Leila: I'd give them a curfew.

Aida: I'd give them more freedom. If they want to go out with their friends, if they like someone, a guy, I would want them to bring him over so I could meet him. . . .

Faida: If I could change one thing, I'd change how the Muslim guys get more freedom than the girls.

Lubna: It's not fair.

Hanaa: I tell my mother that I would let my daughter have more freedom.

Q: And what does she say?

Hanaa: She says, "I don't care what you say just as long as you don't ruin your reputation by doing something."

Curfew: A requirement to be home by a certain time.

Lubna: They think like if you go out you are going to right away go with a guy or do something. A lot of Arab girls aren't allowed out at night. . . .

Salma: I will be so understanding. Have a talk with your kids. There's so much, "I'm going to give you a beating if you do this." If that's what you want to do, fine, go ahead. I'll let them do what they want as long as their name is kept good.

Sina: I go to my room and cry.

Q: You cry?

Sina: Yes, I go to my room and cry because my parents are too strict on me and I'm pretty much limited to things like I don't get to go out at all.

Bahiya: Like cause she had a party.

May: I agree with my parents about 50 percent because it's the culture, but they have to understand that I was practically raised here and have a different way of looking at things than they do, but they never take how I feel and how I am into consideration. Like what they want is the way it's gotta be because that's the Arabic culture and that causes problems.

PARENTS' RESTRICTIONS ON DAUGHTERS

One area of disagreement is the parents' reluctance to let their daughters participate in after-school activities.

Q: What about after-school activities? What if someone wanted to play on a sports team or go out for a play or something like that?

Feryal: I play soccer now. I like it so much. I usually use it as an excuse to get in better shape, to lose weight.

Q: Not all parents will let their daughters stay for after-school activities. What would the school have to do? Is there a concern about boys being present after school? Is that the main concern?

Fatmeh: That's always the concern with them.

Q: What would the school have to do to help?

Fatmeh: The school could call them up and assure them that nothing's going to happen, that I have transportation home.

Q: Then they might consider it?

Amina: I asked my father if I could go out for tennis. You know he thinks tennis, mini-skirts. Shorts are out. You know the uniform *with the guys watching. He doesn't want anyone looking at me. If I go someplace with him, I have to stay in the car.*

Raeda: I can wear shorts so long as it's around the house.

Amet: If we're away, and there are no Arabic people there, it's different. It depends on who's there to see you. . . .

Fanda: My dad, like my sister, was really into sports. He liked that a lot. He went. I wanted to join track and my dad said, fine, he wanted me to. He really likes us to get into things, to do something instead of staying home all the time, but my mother wouldn't let me join. I don't know [if] it's because she went to school here in America and she knows how it is, but she says, "No, I need you at home." I say, "Don't you trust me?" Then she says, "Of course I trust you. It's just that I don't trust anybody else." I mean, come on now.

Q: She worries that someone will take advantage of you?

Fanda: Yeah, and reputation. . . .

PARENTAL TREATMENT OF OLDER AND YOUNGER DAUGHTERS

In some families there is a difference between the treatment of older and younger sisters. Usually this is attributed to an adjustment to American culture on the part of the parents.

Q: Do you have older sisters?

Baloul: Yes.

Q: Was their life different from yours?

Baloul: Yes, very much. We were just talking about that.

Q: How was it different?

Hala: We have a lot more freedom. . . .

Amal: My sister, my parents learned from my sister's experiences. One of my sisters was married when she was fourteen. When my parents came to America, people who were Arabs in America started to say, "Rush off your daughter and get her married because she's going to become Americanized. She'll start smoking," and they brought up the bad side of the American culture. So my parents, they believe it, because they didn't know what was going on in America. So they sent her back to Lebanon and had her married and brought her back here. Now she never got to go to school or got her education or anything, she was a housewife with four kids.

Fadua: I think my mother started putting responsibility on me. I think that was a mistake, when I was seven or eight, that's what I remember. I couldn't go out as much as other kids. She taught me things. She thought she was doing good, and I think that is good, but now I feel that I've missed a lot of my childhood.

Q: Because you didn't get to play as much?

Fadua: Yes, I didn't play as much. I didn't get to run around and jump up and down like kids do. She thought she was doing good. She taught me everything, the housework, everything, because I'm the oldest. Now my little sister is nine, and she is given the freedom to do anything she wants, to go over to her friend's house, have her friends over.

BROTHERS AND SISTERS

There are also differences between families in the influence and responsibility given to brothers in regard to their sisters' behavior. . . .

Q: How do you feel about your brothers and their freedom compared to yours?

Rashida: There are a lot of girls whose brothers tell them what to do, but my mother and father have said to my brothers that what we do does not concern them. Sometimes my older brother will say, "Why are you going there?" And I'll say, "Does that concern you? I'm doing it, not you." But he'll try to tell me because he's protective.

Mona: They're very protective of their sisters. . . .

Q: So [your brother] could say, you can do this or that and this would be okay with your parents?

Nehmeh: Yes, because he's so close to my age that my parents think what he says, he must be right. If he says, don't let her go to this party, well my parents think, well, he's been there, and it must not be good, so you can't go. So that's why I never let him know where I'm going. . . .

Zobeida: My brother helps me. When my parents say no, he says, "Why are you doing this? Let her do this. She's telling you what she's going to do. She's not going to do something else." *(Eisenlohr in Aswad, pp. 254–60)*

Adapting Traditions to Modern Times

From her interviews with Arab American teenagers and their parents, Charlene Eisenlohr found some confusion and inconsistency in the rules parents set for their children. Some rules were different for girls than for boys, and others were different for younger daughters than for older ones when they had been the same age.

Nimat Hafez Barazangi, a Syrian American education professor, studied similar issues relating to Arab American Muslim parents and their children and published her findings in *Arab Americans: Continuity & Change.* She found that it was difficult for these parents to adapt their cultural and religious rules to life in America. One of the rules Barazangi looked at was *hijab,* the Muslim requirement that women be covered, except for their hands and face, whenever they might be seen by a man other than a close relative. The reason for the rule, according to the Koran, is "that they may be known [as believing women] and not molested." One of the fathers Barazangi interviewed explained that, to him, this meant women should dress so that they do not draw attention to themselves. "I feel that my wife or daughter if they go shopping with *hijab,* they'll attract more attention," he concluded. "So I don't force them [to wear *hijab*] because that attracts more attention. But modest dress (not a miniskirt) is a must."

What happened next . . .

Private schools operated by Muslim communities offer Arab American students and parents an atmosphere with fewer cultural conflicts. Since 1980 American Muslim communities have shifted their focus from building mosques (houses of worship) to building schools. In 1989 there were forty-nine Islamic schools in the United States, and by 1998 there were at least two hundred. Between 1995 and 1998 the number of students attending Muslim schools in the New York City area jumped from two hundred to twenty-four hundred.

In addition to classes in subjects like science, mathematics, and social studies, Muslim schools also teach the Arabic language, provide religious instruction, conduct daily prayer services, and recognize events like Ramadan (the Muslim month of fasting) rather than Christian or Jewish holidays

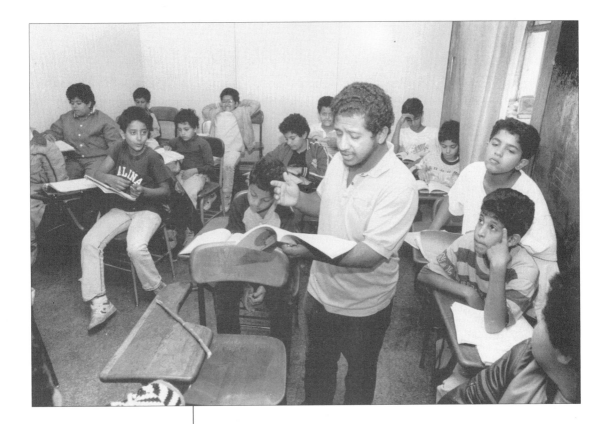

A class at the American Muslim Society in Dearborn, Michigan. The Society has a weekend school in the basement of the mosque in which students study, among other subjects, Arabic and the Koran.

Reproduced by permission of Paul S. Conklin.

like Christmas or Yom Kippur. Boys and girls may attend the same schools, but they do not sit together in the classroom.

Did you know . . .

- Besides dating, Muslim tradition also forbids (or, according to some interpretations, discourages) dancing, smoking, gambling, and drinking alcohol.

- In a study of immigrant Palestinian women that was published in *Family and Gender among American Muslims*, Louise Cainkar found a double standard for dating among Palestinian American girls and boys. Most of the twenty-two women she interviewed said they would "not allow their daughters to date"; they also said they would "not encourage their sons to do so either." One woman explained, "You can't tell boys what to do, they just take their freedom."

- "Sexual virginity at marriage is considered essential for girls," according to Cainkar. "Interestingly, these same women feel that men should have sexual experience before marriage, but they should have it with non-Arab women."

For More Information

Barazangi, Nimat Hafez. "Arab Muslim Identity Transmission: Parents and Youth." *Arab Americans: Continuity & Change.* Edited by Baha Abu-Laban and Michael W. Suleiman. Belmont, MA: Association of Arab-American University Graduates, 1989, pp. 65–82.

Cainkar, Louise. "Immigrant Palestinian Women Evaluate Their Lives." *Family and Gender among American Muslims: Issues Facing Middle Eastern Immigrants and Their Descendants.* Edited by Barbara C. Aswad and Barbara Bilgé. Philadelphia, PA: Temple University Press, 1996, pp. 41–58.

Eisenlohr, Charlene Joyce. "Adolescent Arab Girls in an American High School." *Family and Gender among American Muslims: Issues Facing Middle Eastern Immigrants and Their Descendants.* Edited by Barbara C. Aswad and Barbara Bilgé. Philadelphia, PA: Temple University Press, 1996, pp. 250–70.

Mona

"Mona"

**Selection from *Bint Arab: Arab and Arab American Women
in the United States*, by Evelyn Shakir
Published in 1997**

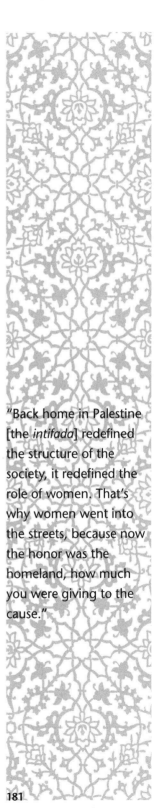

"Back home in Palestine [the *intifada*] redefined the structure of the society, it redefined the role of women. That's why women went into the streets, because now the honor was the homeland, how much you were giving to the cause."

Approximately one-half of Arab Americans are Muslim, and at least 60 percent of recent Arab immigrants belong to that religion. In the Middle East, about 90 percent of Arabs are Muslim, and their cultural traditions are related to their religious beliefs. Most Americans know very little about Islam (the Muslim faith), and what they do know is often distorted, incomplete, or incorrect. One of the sources of greatest confusion is the role of women in Islamic culture. Western feminism asserts that gender (male or female) equality means men and women must be treated the same. Islam teaches that men and women are equal but different. Men are responsible for financially supporting their families, while women bear the main responsibility for raising the children and running the household. Generally, women who want to work outside the home may do so as long as they can also fulfil their family duties.

Another frequently misunderstood aspect of Islam is its requirement that women completely cover themselves in public. Although there are different interpretations of *hijab* (from the Arabic word *hajaba*, meaning "to conceal"), the most common is that women's clothing must cover the entire

Mary Lahaj, a delegate from Massachusetts at the 1988 National Democratic Convention. Lahaj was one of fifty-five Arab American delegates to the 1988 convention; in 1984 there were only four. Arab American women are becoming increasingly active in politics, overcoming the belief of some in the Arab community that if women are politically involved, they may eventually dishonor the family. *Reproduced by permission of Paul S. Conklin.*

body except for the face and hands; it must not be formfitting, sheer, or eye-catching; it must not be similar to men's clothing or to distinctive clothing worn by people of other faiths; and it must not be so fancy or so tattered that it attracts admiration or sympathy. The purpose of *hijab* is not to belittle women but to protect them from unwanted sexual attention. "Anyone who sees [a covered woman] will know that she is a Muslim and has a good moral character," Mary C. Ali noted in her brochure *The Question of Hijab.* "Many Muslim women who cover are filled with dignity and self esteem. . . . As a chaste, modest, pure woman, she does not want her sexuality to enter into interactions with men in the smallest degree."

Evelyn Shakir, a Lebanese American who teaches English at Bentley College near Boston, Massachusetts, wanted to get past the stereotypes and understand what it really meant to be an Arab American woman. In addition to examining her own family life, she interviewed other Arab American women, both Christian and Muslim, and collected their interviews in *Bint Arab: Arab and Arab American Women in the United States.* One of these women, whom she called "Mona," was the daughter of Palestinian immigrants. Unlike the stereotypical Muslim woman, who stays at home and serves her dominant husband, Mona took traditions from both her Arab and American cultures and became the kind of woman she wanted to be.

Things to remember while reading "Mona":

- Although the Muslim religion specifies certain rules for modest dress, the interpretation of those rules varies among Arab countries (all Arab countries are predominantly Muslim, except for Lebanon, which is almost half Christian). Saudi Arabia has some of the most conservative rules, requiring women who are out in public to wear long, loose-fitting dresses; long head scarves that completely cover the hair; and even a veil that covers the face except for the eyes. Some Arabs use the word *hijab* to refer to the custom of covering women except for the face and hands; others use the word to mean only the scarf that covers the hair.

- In 1979, when Mona was nine years old, she and her family visited relatives in Jordan for a month. Her early experience with the *hijab* did not reflect the Islamic ideal: she found that the distinctive clothing encouraged her brother to treat her as an inferior rather than as an equal. As a teenager, Mona essentially created her own form of *hijab* by dressing like a tomboy and not wearing makeup. "I didn't want anything that made me look female or highlighted my gender because I knew that automatically meant restrictions," she told Shakir.

- `According to Muslim tradition, the month called Ramadan is when Muhammad (c. 570–632), the founder of Islam, first received revelations from God. Every year, Muslims use Ramadan for "charging spiritual batteries, for taking time out from the fast lane, for getting to know more about one's creator, one's self and one another," Salam Al-Marayati explained in the *Los Angeles Times*. During this month, Muslims do not eat or drink during daylight hours, and they are encouraged to read the entire Koran (the Muslim holy book).

- The country of Israel was created in 1948 on Palestinian Arab land as a safe haven for Jews. To make room for the new settlers, 780,000 Palestinians were forced from their homes; while about one-half emigrated to the United States or other nations, others sought refuge in nearby lands. Over the next twenty years, Israel conquered more territory belonging to their Arab neighbors, and another 325,000 Arabs were displaced. The *intifada* (in-tay-FAH-dah) was a civil uprising by Palestinians in Israeli-occupied territories. For five years, beginning in late 1987, the Palestinians refused to pay taxes or buy Israeli products, marched in peaceful demonstrations, threw rocks at Israeli soldiers, and occasionally hurled firebombs at Israeli tanks. Palestinian emigrants sent money, food, and medical supplies to support their efforts. Through their participation in the *intifada*, Palestinians developed a sense of pride in their resistance to military conquest.

"Mona"

*[In Jordan] I found my uncle's eight-year-old daughter wearing the **hijab** and a full-length dress. All you could see was her face. And her brothers treated her like [dirt] . . . "Do this! Do that!" But me and my brothers were friends.*

And I remember my uncle was constantly putting down my dad by lecturing him and embarrassing him on how in America he hasn't kept up the culture and the language and especially the religion [Islam].

Hijab: Clothing that covers a Muslim woman's head and body, except for her face and hands.

It was during Ramadan that we went to Jordan, the holy month of fasting. Ramadan was really nice there because the atmosphere is so close and warm. My brother Hassan—he was eleven at the time—he started getting really into the religion and the praying. Me and my brother were very close, so whatever he would do, I wanted to do. My uncle was so happy. "You both want to pray?" But I remember my uncle spending more time with my brother than he would with me, explaining what the prayers meant.

Then, I remember the first time I came to pray with them. I think my arms were showing and my hair was down. My uncle said "Haram [shame]! Go get covered, go get something on your hair, go get something down to here [the wrists]." So I said, "Okay, fine." I went and got the hijab and wore the thing. . . .

At nine you're very impressionable. So when we came back to America, I continued wearing the hijab for about a month. My mom and sister were just very embarrassed and didn't want me to be going out in public. I remember what started turning me off [was] my brother started telling me things like "Well, go get my shoes." He even tried to continue to make me pray behind him. I took it at first, but then I got sick of it all, and I took the hijab off. . . .

I constantly saw the two worlds [Arab and American] clash. But one thing that appealed to me was the freedom Americans got. Freedom and so-called equality that wasn't in our [Arab] culture. [For instance], I was constantly watched. I was constantly told not to hang around with the boys, to be careful of those boys. And you think "What's wrong with those boys?" We biked, we played football, we weren't sitting around playing **spin-the-bottle**. . . .

As time went on, I just started rebelling. "I don't want these restrictions. Why don't you care what my brothers are doing, and why don't you care what time they come home or if they're with girls?"

I was so, so tomboyish. My talk and my manner were very masculine. My hair was just a mess. My clothes were always just either sweats or jeans and an old raggedy T-shirt. It was like I was telling my parents, "I don't have any sexuality, so you don't have to worry about me." . . .

I carried that tomboyish look and attitude up until, I'd say, age eighteen. At eighteen I started to come to terms with it's okay to be female. You do have sexuality, you do have feelings, you do get attracted to men and vice versa; but at the same time, you are still a

Spin-the-bottle: A kissing game.

person and you can do whatever you want without all the restrictions of being "female." . . .

I never really was involved in politics until I was sixteen and I went to a picnic of a Palestinian organization. At first, I didn't want to go because I thought they would all be like the people from my village.

But when I [got there], I was totally shocked. You had all these youths from fifteen to thirty, and everybody was just so socially open. You had males and females, mothers and fathers, all sitting together like one family, all laughing together and playing together, and some of the younger men and women were playing volleyball, and some were in their bathing suits, going to go swimming. I didn't know there were Arabs and Arab Americans like this. I felt like this was where I belonged.

From then on, I became involved [with this Palestinian club]. I was going back and forth to the Palestinian community center, and my family were so relieved and so happy that I was getting back in touch with the Arab culture and identity. But I was still tough, and the men viewed me as tough. I didn't leave any room for flirting. . . .

My junior year in high school, the **intifada** broke out, and my involvement just took off! . . .

Every day after school let out, I would automatically go to the club, to organize, prepare posters, call people, and then take off and go demonstrate. Now I became "Palestinian," period. I wouldn't even let anybody call me "Palestinian American." I would love when somebody would say, "She's more Palestinian than the people from back home." That was the best.

I still denied my femininity and sexuality because I wanted to let everyone know that when I leave the house it's for politics, nothing else. Because they [the Arab community] think if women are politically involved, then they will have easy contacts to men, politics will lead into a friendship and then into a relationship, automatically sexual and automatically dishonoring the family. So I wanted to prove to them that I was sincere, I wasn't trying to use politics as a means to an end, a way to meet men or a way to get out of the house. And all the time, my parents were telling me, "We're Arab, and Arab girls are not like this [public and active]." . . .

But then as time went on, I started realizing that being Arab doesn't mean just what they mean. I found my honor through my

Intifada: A civilian resistance movement by Palestinians against the Israeli government.

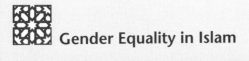

Gender Equality in Islam

Before the time of Muhammad (c. 570–632), the founder of Islam, the Arab world consisted of various tribes that each treated women differently. In some tribes, women were treated as well as men; in others, they were treated as possessions, and female infants were often killed. The Koran (also spelled Qur'an), which Muslims believe contains God's revelations to Muhammad, includes many statements about the equal dignity of men and women, and it orders men not to mistreat women.

Interpretations of the Koran vary, just as interpretations of the Bible vary among Christian denominations and interpretations of the Torah vary among Jewish groups. The Koran was written in Arabic, and translators often choose different words when writing modern English versions. These choices can introduce changes in meaning, so Muslims are encouraged to learn Arabic and read the scriptures in their original form. As a result of these interpretations, some people claim Muslims believe women are inferior to men, while many Muslims maintain this is not true.

In his paper "Women in the Qur'an and the Sunnah," Abdur Rahman I. Doi wrote that the Koran tells men to "live with [women] on a footing of kindness and equity." The Koran also states, "Women are the twin halves of men." Doi explained that some passages of the Koran give men rights over women, but that other passages give women similar rights over men.

In her article "American, Ambitious, and Muslim," Shaheen Ahmed described a woman who had recently converted to Islam. Formerly a Southern Baptist, this twenty-three-year-old medical student said, "The right to vote, to work outside the home, to [receive] inheritance are things that women in this country did not even have until the 1920s, but Muslims had for much longer."

In the 1980 article "Women in the Arab World," Nouha al-Hegelan wrote, "Many American women in the past several years have sought to keep their maiden names after marriage. This tradition has been enjoyed by Islamic women for centuries, and rightly so. After all, the wife is one of a pair, a couple—terms literally conveying equality. In fact, the Arabic word for wife, 'Alzawja,' literally means 'one of a pair.'"

political work. And that was [because of] the intifada, *too. I mean, back home in Palestine it redefined the structure of the society, it redefined the role of women. That's why women went into the streets, because now the honor was the homeland, how much you were giving to the cause, not the woman's sexuality. . . .*

I'm a political leader in the community; I'm looked upon as a leader for the youth. So I'm out to prove, not just for other people but also for myself, that as females we can do it all and still keep our respect. (Mona in Shakir, pp. 160-64)

What happened next . . .

When she was younger, Mona hated to be called "Arab American." She thought it meant she was neither a good Arab nor a good American. But as she became secure in her identity, she realized it really meant having "the best of both worlds." "Politically, as [Arab Americans], we know how to work with the mainstream and do outreach; we have an advantage over the Arabs back home," she told Shakir.

On the subject of dating, Mona and her parents agreed on a compromise between Arab and American customs. "I will not date just to date," she said. "But if [someone is] interested in a commitment, and he thinks that I might fit the bill, if he's looking for a sincere relationship and not just a good time, then we'll explore, we'll get to know each other. . . . And my family will be automatically involved."

Did you know . . .

- In the United States, about 70 percent of the people who convert to Islam are women. Many of them are well-educated professionals. Some of them wear traditional *hijab* clothing, while others cover themselves with contemporary clothing and scarves.

- It is only necessary for a Muslim woman to cover herself completely if she might be seen by a man other than a close family member, like her husband, brother, or father. At home with her family, or with female friends, she can dress more casually.

- The Koran also requires Muslim men to dress modestly. For example, a man must be covered from his navel to his knees; he may not wear tight, sheer, or eye-catching clothing; he may not wear women's clothing or distinctive clothing worn by members of other faiths; and he may not wear silk garments or gold jewelry. Women, however, may wear silk and gold.

For More Information

Ahmed, Shaheen. "American, Ambitious, and Muslim." Available at http://www.geocities.com/Wellesley/3321/win8b.htm (May 1999).

Al-Hegelan, Nouha. "Women in the Arab World." *Arab Perspectives,* October 1980. Available on the Ethnic Woman International Web site at http://www.thefuturesite.com/ethnic/arab.html (May 1999).

Ali, Mary C. *The Question of Hijab: Suppression or Liberation?* A brochure published by the Institute of Islamic Information and Education, Chicago, IL. Available at http://www.usc.edu/dept/MSA/humanrelations/womeninislam/whatishijab.html (May 1999).

Al-Marayati, Salam. "Ramadan: Fasting for Spiritual Reflection, Renewal." *Los Angeles Times,* January 11, 1997. Available at http://www.mpac.org/opinion/art007.html (May 1999).

Doi, Abdur Rahman I. "Women in the Qur'an and the Sunnah." Available at http://www.beconvinced.com/women/Q_S.htm (June 1999).

Shakir, Evelyn. *Bint Arab: Arab and Arab American Women in the United States.* Westport, CT: Praeger, 1997.

Lisa Suhair Majaj

"Boundaries: Arab/American"

Selection from *Food for Our Grandmothers*, edited by Joanna Kadi
Published in 1994

Lisa Suhair Majaj's father was a Palestinian Arab, and her mother was an American of German heritage. While Majaj was growing up in Jordan, she was an American Arab who had relatively fair skin, light hair, and little knowledge of Arabic. When she came to the United States in 1982, at the age of twenty-two, Majaj became an Arab American who had relatively dark skin and Arab facial features, spoke English with an accent, and belonged to an ethnic group that many Americans thought of as uncivilized and violent. She felt she did not fit into either society.

Majaj was born in Iowa, her mother's home. Her father had come to the United States to attend college after the country of Israel was established as a Jewish homeland, on Palestinian Arab lands, in 1948. In the Middle East he had fought to keep the new Jewish nation from taking Palestinian land; in the United States he faced racial prejudice because he spoke with an accent and people thought he looked Jewish. Because this prejudice limited his job opportunities, he took his wife and two small daughters to Jordan. Majaj's father was frustrated because he could not move back to his hometown,

> "Being American in the Arab world set me apart in ways I found profoundly disturbing. But I discovered soon enough that being Arab in the United States—worse, being Palestinian—offers little in the way of reassurance."

Two Arab American women walking down a New York street, April 1993. Arab countries are predominantly Muslim, and Muslim women are expected to cover all parts of their body except their hands and face and to cover their hair with a scarf. *Reproduced by permission of AP/Wide World Photos.*

which now belonged to Israel. Her mother also missed her home in America. "I learned to live as if in a transitional state, waiting always for the time that we would go to Palestine, to the United States, to a place where I would belong," Majaj wrote in "Boundaries: Arab/American." "But trips to Iowa and to Jerusalem taught me that once I got there, 'home' slipped away inexplicably [mysteriously], materializing again just beyond reach."

In Jordan, Majaj was treated like a foreigner. In accord with traditional Arab gender (male and female) roles, Majaj's father was primarily responsible for supporting the family financially, while her mother was mostly responsible for raising the children. "I grew up reading Mother Goose, singing 'Home on the Range,' reciting 'The Ride of Paul Revere,' and drawing pictures of Pilgrims and Indians, Christmas trees and Santa Clauses, Valentines and Easter bunnies," she wrote. Although she took some classes in Arabic, she never became fluent. Her parents spoke English at home, and she attended American schools in Amman, the capital of Jordan.

In America, Majaj was also treated like a foreigner. Most Americans could not understand why Palestinians refused to make peace with Israel, even though they had been driven from homes that had belonged to their families for generations. Aside from those who were resisting Israeli occupation of their land, virtually the only Palestinians that Americans saw in television and newspaper reports were terrorists who were taking hostages, hijacking airplanes, or blowing up buildings. (A terrorist is a person who uses violence or threats to frighten or intimidate a group or government into giving into the terrorist's demands, usually political.) So when Majaj's new acquaintances in America found out she was Palestinian, they felt uncomfortable. She tried to avoid such problems by not talking about her background. "Silence made it possible for me to blend into my surroundings, chameleon-like," she wrote in "Boundaries: Arab/American." "But its implications were disastrous. Silence wrapped itself around my limbs like cotton wool, wound itself into my ears and eyes, filled my mouth and muffled my throat. I do not know at what point I began to choke. Perhaps there was never a single incident, just a slow deposition [layering] of sediment over time. Until one day, retching, I spat out some unnameable substance. And I attempted to speak."

Majaj came to the United States to study English literature and American culture. It was natural for her to choose writing as one of the ways she could speak about her background and her struggle to reconcile her two identities. She has become an award-winning poet, and her essays have been published in several collections.

Things to remember while reading "Boundaries: Arab/American":

- When Majaj came to the United States, she confronted several of the stereotypical images Americans associate with Palestinian Arabs. One is that Palestinians often carry "kalashnikovs" (Russian-made submachine guns), either to fight Israelis or to commit acts of terrorism.

- Another stereotype is that Arab women wear veils, submit passively to their domineering husbands, and remain silent in public. Arab countries are predominantly Muslim, and Muslim women are expected to cover all parts of their body except their hands and face and to cover their hair with a scarf: Saudi Arabia is the only Arab country that requires women to wear veils over their faces. Muslim women often have careers; in a 1996 survey of American Muslim women, more than one-half said they worked outside the home.

- Majaj not only looked foreign in Jordan, but she also acted foreign. It was not considered proper for an Arab girl to walk around the city by herself. An Arab man once told her, "You don't walk like an Arab girl. You take long steps; there's a bounce to your stride." The man was criticizing her lack of appropriate femininity, but Majaj recalled that she hoped it meant "that perhaps I was, after all, American."

"Boundaries: Arab/American"

*When I arrived in the United States for graduate school in 1982, I felt oddly invisible. Walking down the crowded streets of Ann Arbor, Michigan I became aware, with a mixture of relief and unease, that no one was looking at me, trying to talk to me, or making comments under their breath. Years of living in Jordan and Lebanon, where my physical appearance, my style of dressing, my manner of walking had all coded me as foreign, had accustomed me to being the object of attention, curiosity, and sometimes harassment. Although in Amman [Jordan] and Beirut [Lebanon] I had tried to make myself as **inconspicuous** as possible—walking close to walls, never meeting anyone's eyes—I always knew that people noted, **assessed**, commented on my presence. Even as I disliked and resented this attention, I grew to expect it. As a girl and woman with little self-confidence, the external gaze, **intrusive** as it was, perhaps offered the **solace** of definition: I am seen, therefore I exist. Without that gaze would I still know who I was? . . .*

Inconspicuous: Unnoticeable; invisible.

Assessed: Analyzed.

Intrusive: Unwelcome.

Solace: Comfort.

*Being American in the Arab world set me apart in ways I found **profoundly** disturbing. But I discovered soon enough that being Arab in the United States—worse, being Palestinian—offers little in the way of **reassurance.** My hopeful belief that moving to the United States would be a homecoming was quickly shaken. Once I claimed a past, spoke my history, told my name, the walls of **incomprehension** and hostility rose, brick by brick: un-funny "ethnic" jokes, jibes about **terrorists** and **kalashnikovs,** about veiled women and camels; or worse, the awkward silences, the hasty shifts to other subjects. Searching for images of my Arab self in American culture I found only unrecognizable **stereotypes.** . . .*

When I walked down the streets of Amman I was categorized as foreign, female; a target of curiosity and harassment. My appearance alone in public and my foreignness seemed to suggest sexual availability; whispers of charmoota, *prostitute, echoed in my burning ears. The **insidious** touch of young men's hands on my body pursued me, their eyes taunting me in mock innocence when I whirled to confront them. Once, when a young man crowded me against a wall, brushing my hips with his hand as he passed, I cried out wildly and swung my bag at him. But he advanced threateningly toward me, shouting angrily at my **effrontery.** If I had spoken Arabic to him he might have retreated in shame. Because I did not he must have seen me simply as a foreign woman, flaunting a sexuality **unmediated** by the protection of men, the uncles and brothers and cousins whom an Arab woman would be assumed to have. . . .*

*As walking became a measure of my independence, it became as well a measure of our conflict of wills. [My father] did not like my "wandering in the streets"; it was not "becoming," and it threatened his own honor. I stole away for walks, therefore, during the drowsy hours after the heavy midday meal when most people, my father included, were either at work or at **siesta.** Walking in the early afternoon, especially during the summer months, **accentuated** my difference from the Jordanian culture I had determined to resist. A young woman walking quickly and alone through still, hot streets, past drowsy guards and bored shopkeepers, presented an **anomaly:** Arab girls, I had been told both **subtly** and **explicitly,** did not do such things—a fact that pleased me.*

As my sister and I entered the "dangerous age," when our reputations were increasingly at stake and a wrong move would brand us as "loose," my father grew more and more rigid in his efforts to regulate our self-definitions. Our options in life were spelled out in

Profoundly: Deeply.

Reassurance: Comfort.

Incomprehension: Not understanding.

Terrorist: A person who uses violence or threats to frighten or intimidate a group or government into giving in to the terrorist's demands, usually political.

Kalishnikovs: Russian-made submachine guns.

Stereotypes: Simple and inaccurate images of the members of a particular racial or ethnic group.

Insidious: Sneaky.

Effrontery: Boldness.

Unmediated: Unassisted.

Siesta: Afternoon nap.

Accentuated: Brought attention to; pointed out.

Anomaly: Oddity; something out of the ordinary.

Subtly: Quietly.

Explicitly: Clearly.

*terms of whom we would be permitted to marry. A Palestinian Christian, I knew, was the preferred choice. . . . To marry an American, or Britisher, or Canadian was out of the question. Westerners, I heard repeatedly, had no **morals**, no respect for family, no sense of honor—an opinion that seemed to **derive** in part from observations of real cultural differences between Arabs and westerners, in part from the weekly episodes of **Peyton Place** and other English-language programs aired on Jordan television. (I have been asked by Arabs whether Americans really get divorces six or seven times, abandon their elderly parents, and are all wealthy. And I have been asked by Americans whether Arabs really ride camels to work, live in tents, and have never seen planes or hospitals.). . . .*

*This exploration [reading feminist writers] reinforced my **acute** awareness of the representation and misrepresentation of Arab culture in the United States. There are ways in which Palestinian women escape the typical stereotypes of Arab women—exotic, sensualized, victimized—only to be laden with the more male-coded, or perhaps merely **generic**, images of irrational terrorists and **pathetic** refugees. But none of these images reflect the Arab women I know: my widowed Palestinian grandmother, who raised three boys and buried two girls, raising two grandchildren as well after their mother was killed by a **Zionist** group's bomb, whose strength and independence people still speak of with awe; or my Lebanese aunt, a skilled nurse who ran a Jerusalem hospital ward for years, raised four children, gracefully met the social requirements of her husband's busy political and medical careers, and now directs a center for disabled children. My increasing anger at the portrayal of the Middle East as a chaotic realm outside the boundaries of rational Western comprehension, and a slowly developing confidence in my own political and cultural knowledge, came together with my **burgeoning** feminism to make possible an **articulation** that, although **tentative**, was more **empowering** than anything I had experienced. (Majaj in Kadi, pp. 66-67, 76-78, 80-81)*

What happened next . . .

In Jordan Majaj was most aware of her American nature, but in the United States she became more conscious of

Morals: Values; sense of right or wrong.

Derive: Develop.

Peyton Place: A prime-time soap opera.

Acute: Sharp.

Generic: Generalized.

Pathetic: Worthy of pity.

Zionist: A person who believes in the establishment and development of the Jewish state of Israel.

Burgeoning: Budding; developing.

Articulation: Expression; personal statement.

Tentative: Unsure; cautious.

Empowering: Strengthening.

her Arab self. For example, although the Jordanian culture in the 1970s saw a certain amount of body weight as evidence of prosperity and social status, Majaj wanted to be thin like the models she saw in American magazines like *Seventeen.* In fact, she suffered from anorexia (a compulsion to become excessively thin) for several years; even as she struggled with her eating disorder, she was ashamed that she was embarrassing her family by being so skinny.

Majaj overcame her anorexia and regained her health, but she still struggled with her identity. After she moved to America, one of her friends was an Arab from Egypt. This friend once told her that she had recognized Majaj as an Arab the moment they met: she could tell by the fullness of Majaj's lips. "It was the first time I'd thought of myself as being identifiably Arab, and I felt a sudden sense of relief: at last another Arab had claimed me as kin," Majaj wrote in "The Body, in Several Languages." "My body that had always made me feel alien in the Middle East seemed more homelike after that."

Identity and Language

As a child, Lisa Suhair Majaj learned just enough conversational Arabic to talk a little with her grandmother. But she could not participate in conversations at family gatherings, understand Arabic radio or television programs, read newspapers, or even talk to store clerks. She had no Arab friends. Her father wanted her to speak Arabic, but when she took lessons, he became frustrated with their slow conversations and preferred to talk with her in English. During her early twenties, Majaj tried again to learn Arabic, but, as she commented in "Boundaries: Arab/American," "I must have harbored more internal resistance to learning Arabic than I then realized."

Knowing that one of the best ways to understand a culture is to speak its language, Majaj has continued to try to learn Arabic. In "The Body, in Several Languages" she wrote, "Although my Arabic competency remains tentative, the sounds so difficult to English speakers emerge passably from deep in my throat. This language which should have been mine seems to lie waiting for me to claim it."

Did you know . . .

- As a teenager, Majaj's sister, who was three years older than Majaj, had a figure like an American fashion model. Her Palestinian relatives constantly urged her to gain weight.

- Contrary to her father's wishes, Majaj married a Greek citizen of Cyprus (an island in the Mediterranean Sea). By this time, she was proud of her Arab heritage, and she decided to keep her Arab name rather than take her husband's last name.

- Majaj's religion also made her feel like an outsider in Jordan. She and her family are Christians, but 95 percent of Jordanians are Muslim. About 7 percent of the world's six million Palestinians are Christian. Many of them have left the Middle East because the Jewish government limits the rights of non-Jews to own land or build homes and businesses in Israel. In Jerusalem, which is now the capital of Israel, one-half the population was Christian in 1922; by the late 1990s, less than 2 percent of Jerusalem's residents were Christian.

For More Information

Majaj, Lisa Suhair. "The Body, in Several Languages." *absinthe,* January 1997. Available at http://www.acs.ucalgary.ca/~amathur/majaj.html (June 1999).

Majaj, Lisa Suhair. "Boundaries: Arab/American." *Food for Our Grandmothers: Writings by Arab-American and Arab-Canadian Feminists.* Edited by Joanna Kadi. Boston, MA: South End Press, 1994, pp. 65–84.

Religion in
Arab American Communities

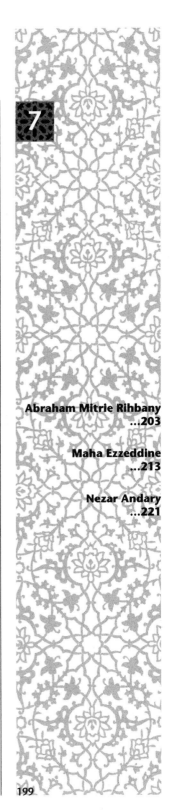

7

Having left the physical familiarity of their home country and the emotional familiarity of their relatives and friends, immigrants often turn to their faith for comfort and security in their new country. At least 90 percent of the first-wave Arab immigrants to America were Christians, and they looked for churches that were as similar as possible to the ones they had left behind. For example, many Syrian Orthodox immigrants (about one-half of the early Arab immigrants) attended Russian Orthodox churches until they could establish their own Arab congregations. Arab Catholics (Maronites and Melkites) attended Roman Catholic churches; only about one-half of them later returned to ethnic congregations. Fewer than 3 percent of the early Arab immigrants were Protestants; **Abraham Mitrie Rihbany**, who came to America in 1891, had originally been a member of the Syrian (Greek) Orthodox Church but had been converted by Presbyterian missionaries in Syria.

Islam (the Muslim faith) was originally an Arab religion; it was founded during the seventh century in what is now Saudi Arabia. The Arab world is now more than 90 per-

Friction among Religious Factions

The Turkish Ottoman Empire controlled the Arab world for four hundred years, ending in 1918. "True to the motto 'divide and conquer' [the Turks] kept the Moslems and Christians at odds with each other," Syrian American historian Philip Kayal (1943–) explained in *Arabic Speaking Communities in American Cities.* "Hoping to gain a foothold in the area, the French supported the Maronites and the Russians cultivated ties with the Greek [Syrian] Orthodox faithful whose religion they shared. The English often assisted the Melkites and Druse." Especially in Lebanon, which has an unusually diverse population for an Arab country (approximately 60 percent Muslim, 30 percent Christian, and 10 percent Druze), tensions still exist among these religious factions.

Arab immigrants brought their ethnic and religious rivalries with them to the United States. But since 1975, a Lebanese civil war, other Middle Eastern wars, and a series of terrorist incidents have focused negative attention on Arab Americans. (A terrorist is a person who uses violence or threats to frighten or intimidate a group or government into giving in to the terrorist's demands, usually political.) This has encouraged them to place less emphasis on their religious differences and view themselves more as a single community.

cent Muslim; only two Arab countries have Muslim populations lower than 90 percent: the Sudan has about 75 percent and Lebanon has less than 60 percent. In the United States, approximately one-half of the Arab American population is Muslim, and the rest are Christian. Islam is the fastest-growing religion in the United States; by the year 2000 there were more American Muslims than American Presbyterians, Episcopalians, or Mormons, and about the same number as American Jews. A small but conspicuous group called the Nation of Islam, led by Louis Farrakhan, has a different set of beliefs, and other Muslims do not consider it a true Islamic religion.

Muslim Arabs initially hesitated to move to a predominantly Christian country, fearing that they would not be able to practice their religion freely and that the social atmosphere would conflict with their moral values. The second and third waves of Arab immigrants, however, have been approximately 60 percent Muslim. By 1990 there were about 620,000

Muslim Arab Americans, which represented 12 percent of the American Muslim population of five million. As the Muslim population became more sizable, people like **Maha Ezzeddine** felt freer and more compelled to explain their beliefs and experiences to other Americans.

The vast majority of Arab immigrants have been either Christian or Muslim. A few, however, have been members of the Druze (sometimes spelled "Druse") faith, which is rooted in the Islamic tradition but is not accepted by mainstream Muslims. Worldwide, there are approximately 500,000 Druze, with around 25,000 living in the United States. The Druze consider religion a private, even secret matter, which is difficult to sustain in a society in which many different religious groups freely discuss and actively promote their beliefs. Since the 1970s a reform movement has developed among American Druze who are concerned about their young people losing contact with their religion; the movement stresses an increased sense of involvement in the Druze community as well as greater access to information about the faith (for members and for the general public). **Nezar Andary**, a young Druze leader, has become a spokesman for this movement.

For More Information

Kayal, Philip M. "Religion in the Christian 'Syrian-American Community.'" *Arabic Speaking Communities in American Cities*. Edited by Barbara C. Aswad. New York: Center for Migration Studies, 1974, pp. 111–36.

Abraham Mitrie Rihbany

A Far Journey
**Excerpts from the autobiography of Abraham Mitrie Rihbany
Published in 1914**

Abraham Mitrie Rihbany (1869–1944) was born into a Greek Orthodox family in a small Syrian village. As a teenager, to get a good education, he attended a Presbyterian boarding school about ten miles away. At that time, the Catholic and Orthodox Churches relied more on ritual and emotion and actually discouraged their members from reading the Bible. Rihbany was an intellectually curious young man, and the Protestant approach to reading the Bible and discussing Christian beliefs appealed to him. While attending the school, he left the Orthodox Church and became a Protestant Christian.

Rihbany learned about the United States in his boarding school, which was operated by American missionaries. He also met several Syrians who had gone to work in America for a few years and returned home with large amounts of money. In 1891, when he was twenty-two, Rihbany heard that two of his friends were about to leave for America, and he decided to go with them.

A year and a half after arriving in the United States, Rihbany decided he would never learn the English language

"It was in that Presbyterian school on the western slopes of my native Lebanon that I first learned to think of Christianity as a personal and not a corporate religion."

or American customs if he stayed in the Syrian community in New York City. He began traveling around the Midwest, earning money by giving speeches about the Holy Land (which was then part of Syria) to churches and community groups. At first, his English was so poor he was barely able to make himself understood. But as he talked with people and listened to church sermons (sometimes following along in his Arabic Bible and sometimes in an English text), his skill with the language quickly improved. Even though he had no formal training as a preacher, he was occasionally invited to deliver a sermon at one of the churches he visited.

In 1896 the members of a Congregational church in Morenci, Michigan, liked his sermon so much they asked him to become their pastor. His lack of training made him reluctant, so he agreed only to serve them for a few weeks before going back to the lecture tour. But when he returned after the tour, they still wanted him to be their permanent pastor, and he finally accepted. After three years at the Morenci church, he served churches in Mount Pleasant, Michigan, for two years and in Toledo, Ohio, for nine years. In 1911 he became pastor of the Church of the Disciples, a Congregational church in Boston, Massachusetts. Rihbany was frequently invited to speak to groups about his life, and in 1912 the *Atlantic Monthly* magazine published a series of articles he wrote about his Syrian and American experiences. Expanding on these articles, he wrote his autobiography, *A Far Journey,* which was published in 1914.

Things to remember while reading the excerpts from *A Far Journey:*

- Rihbany's parents belonged to the Greek Orthodox Church. In 1054 A.D. the Catholic Church split, largely over a difference of belief about the authority of the pope, the Church's leader. One part became the Eastern Orthodox Church, and the other became the Roman Catholic Church, which retained the pope as its head. Within the Eastern Orthodox Church, various ethnic branches developed, including the Greek Orthodox Church. Beginning in the sixteenth century, some groups within the Roman Catholic Church broke away to form various Protestant Christian churches.

- Christmas did not become a Christian feast (day of celebration) until 336 A.D., when Christians in the Roman Empire began celebrating the birth of Jesus Christ on December 25, probably to compete with a pagan feast celebrating the birth of the sun god. During the following 150 years, the celebration of Christmas spread throughout the Christian world. Middle Eastern Christian churches had traditionally celebrated the feast of the Epiphany (literally, "appearance") as the "birth" of Christ because they believed he became divine at the moment of his baptism.

- Muslim Turks established the Ottoman Empire about 1200 A.D., eventually conquering much of the eastern Mediterranean region. The empire controlled Syria from 1516 until 1918.

A Far Journey
The Religion of My Fathers

*The feasts and festivals of the Greek [Orthodox] Church filled my boyish heart with delight, so spectacular and so full of mystery were they. The Syrian churches do not make much of **Christmas** because originally it was not an **Oriental** holiday. New Year's, or "Good-Morning Day," as the Syrians call it, was the day when we exchanged presents and indulged in much gayety. But what was of absorbing interest to me as a boy, aside from the few **coppers** and sugar-plums that I got for presents, was the offering I carried to the fountain, early on New Year's morning. My older sisters went with their jars to carry water for the household, and I went with them. We took with us a few handfuls of wheat and cereals and cast them reverently into the water, saying "Good-morning, fountain! Bless and increase our grain!" So did we ignorantly practice the modes of worship of our remote Oriental ancestors, who poured their gifts to **Astarte** into the streams of Syria ages before Christianity was born. . . .*

*But what was all that compared to the feast of Epiphany, which we celebrated in commemoration of the baptism of Jesus in the river Jordan, twelve days after Christmas? It is known to the people as El-Gitas (dipping in water). I was taught to believe, and most joyously did believe, that the rivers and fountains of the entire world became suddenly holy about sunset on the eve of Epiphany. Wild beasts left not their dens the entire night, and were all **rendered** harmless as doves, because the Christ was on his way to the Jordan. . . .*

The material feast of Epiphany was zulabiah (fried cakes of the doughnut variety). I do not remember that I ever was unwilling to

Christmas: The feast day commemorating the birth of Jesus Christ.

Oriental: Eastern.

Coppers: Copper coins.

Astarte: The principal goddess of certain ancient Middle Eastern cultures.

Rendered: Made.

do any errand for my mother which served to further the cause of "frying" on that sacred occasion. The zulabiah *must* be fried in pure olive oil over a fire of olive wood, whenever it could be obtained, for the olive is the most sacred among the trees. It was supreme joy to me to feed the fire while my mother fried the cakes, to see the bars, coils, and balls of dough swell and sizzle in the hot oil, and to watch my mother take them out of the frying-pan, brown and hissing, and drop them into a large basin of grape molasses. A choice quantity of zulabiah *we gave to the priest, when he came with his attendant on Epiphany day and sprinkled **holy water** at the door and in the four corners of the house, with an olive branch tied to a small cross. . . .*

*I was born into my faith; and my faith was ready-made for me. The **confessional, fasts,** and **sacraments** of the Church met my every need. **Reasoning** about religion was never known to my forefathers, and I was not supposed to go so far as to **indulge** in it. But I did, and that early in my youth. Early in my youth I felt the inward urgency to reason, not only within the **tenets** of my faith, but about and beyond them. But the atmosphere of my early life was not favorable to such modes of thinking. Therefore, my battling with the issues of religion had to be postponed to a later time. . . .*

At the Temple Gate

*Having departed from the Greek Church in my youth, I carried away with me from that fold not **doctrines**, but religious feelings. My Mother Church **exerted** upon me **unconscious, mystic,** indefinable spiritual influences. In the almost entire absence of preaching in that church doctrines are only **implied** in the **ritual**, not directly taught to the **laity**. As a Greek Orthodox, I simply took it for granted that the tenets of the faith of my church were absolutely correct.*

*When I first came in contact with Protestantism in the American mission school at Sûk-el-Gharb, that faith appealed to me as a more stimulating, more enlightened, and more enlightening form of the Christian religion than the one into which I was born. It was the intellectual and **ethical** phases of Protestantism which drew me away from the less reflective faith of my fathers. . . .*

*To my Mother Church, the Greek Orthodox, I am indebted for the earliest spiritual inspiration which flowed into my life in the name of Christ. Notwithstanding the **pagan** traits which still cling to her,*

Holy water: Water that has been blessed by a priest.

Confessional: A small booth in which a person tells his or her sins to a priest, who forgives those sins on behalf of God.

Fasts: Periods during which people limit what they eat and drink, often for religious purposes.

Sacraments: Certain religious acts Christians believe were established by Jesus.

Reasoning: Analyzing; intellectualizing.

Indulge: Take part; give in to.

Tenets: Beliefs.

Doctrines: Religious teachings.

Exerted: Forced.

Unconscious: Unquestionable.

Mystic: Mysterious; supernatural.

Implied: Hinted at.

Ritual: Traditional act.

Laity: Non-clergy.

Ethical: Pertaining to the study of ethics, or of what's right and wrong.

Pagan: Ancient religions with many gods.

that ancient church fixed my eyes in childhood and youth upon the cross of Christ as symbol of the soul's victory over sin and death.

*To the missionary zeal of the great Presbyterian denomination, and to its firmness in the Christian faith as it is known to its members, I am indebted for my first lessons in the religion of an open Bible, and of individual **conviction**. It was in that Presbyterian school on the western slopes of my native Lebanon that I first learned to think of Christianity as a personal and not a **corporate** religion.*

*To the Methodist Episcopal Church of America I owe the **profoundest** sense of spiritual **fervor**. In my lonely days of poverty and struggle, when America was yet a strange land to me, the brotherly spirit and friendly touch of Methodism did more than any other one church influence to renew my strength and steady my **faltering** steps. . . .*

*To the Congregational Church, both Trinitarian and Unitarian, I owe the largest measure of **theological** freedom and the highest level of spiritual thought I have yet attained. . . .*

Now, do you wish to know what riches I have gathered in the New World? I will tell you. These are my riches, which neither moth nor rust can corrupt. I have traveled from the primitive social life of a Syrian village to a great city which embodies the noblest traditions of the most enlightened country in the world. I have come from the bondage of Turkish rule to the priceless heritage of American citizenship. Though one of the least of her loyal citizens, I am rich in the sense that I am helping in my small way to solve America's great problems and to realize her wondrous possibilities. In this great country I have been taught to believe in and to labor for an enlightened and cooperative individualism, universal peace, free churches, and free schools. I have journeyed from the religion of "authority for truth" to the religion of "truth for authority"—a religion which teaches me the fatherhood of God, the brotherhood of man and the friendliness of the universe, and makes me heir to all the prayers, songs, and sermons of the ages. (Rihbany, A Far Journey, *pp. 93–94, 96–97, 102–03, 324–25, 342–46)*

Conviction: Belief.

Corporate: Relating to a group of individuals.

Profoundest: Deepest.

Fervor: Devotion; zeal.

Faltering: Stumbling.

Theological: Relating to the study of God.

Traditional Arab Christian Churches

During the early years of Arab immigration, there were few Syrian churches in the United States. Many of the immigrants joined American churches that seemed most similar to their traditional beliefs and practices. Some remained with their new churches, while others stayed only until they could organize Syrian congregations.

Arab immigrants who were Orthodox Christians tended to join the Episcopal Church. In 1895 the first Orthodox parish for Arab immigrants was organized in New York City. Some Orthodox communities continued to use the Aramaic language (a pre-Arabic language spoken by Jesus) in their ceremonies; these are now part of the Syrian Orthodox Church, whose headquarters are in Damascus, Syria. Others began using English in their services; they now make up the Antiochian Orthodox Church in North America. In 1990 there were 22 Syrian Orthodox parishes and 170 Antiochian Orthodox communities in the United States.

The Melkite Church is a branch of the Eastern Orthodox Church that rejoined the Roman Catholic Church in 1724. Melkite priests from Syria arrived in the United States in 1889 and organized parishes in New York and Chicago, Illinois. The first Melkite bishop in America was appointed in 1966. By the 1990s there were 42 Melkite communities in the United States with a total membership of 75,000.

The Maronite Church is a Syrian branch of the Roman Catholic Church. The Aramaic language is used for church services. There are approximately 150,000 Maronite Catholics in 62 communities in the United States.

The Chaldean Church is an Iraqi branch of the Roman Catholic Church. Services are conducted in Aramaic. The first U.S. parish was established in Chicago in 1934. There are 100,000 members in 14 parishes in the United States.

The Coptic Orthodox Church is based in Egypt. The first communities were established in the United States in the late 1960s. By the 1990s there were 29 Coptic Orthodox churches in the United States.

What happened next . . .

During his twenty-seven years as pastor of the Church of the Disciples, Rihbany wrote nine books, including his 1914 autobiography, *A Far Journey,* which was reprinted in 1925 and 1931. His most popular book, *The Syrian Christ,* was a biography of Jesus; first published in 1916, it was reprinted seven times. A translation of *The Syrian Christ* was published three times in Germany between 1928 and 1962. Rihbany also wrote a children's version of the story, which was published in 1916 and 1923.

Some of Rihbany's books, like *Seven Days with God,* were primarily spiritual in nature. Others presented his knowledge and opinions about the Middle East. For example, *The Hidden Treasure of Rasmola* is about Syrian social life and customs, and *Wise Men from the East and from the West* compares the religious and social attitudes of people from Arab and American cultures. In *Militant America and Jesus Christ,* he examined the religious implications of World War I (1914–18), and in *America Save the Near East,* he expressed his views about Western involvement in Syrian politics.

Did you know . . .

- In 1892 Rihbany became the first literary editor of *Kawkab Amirka* (Star of America), the first Arabic-language newspaper published in North America. His outspoken editorials about Syrian politics irritated the harsh and repressive Turkish government. Because many of the paper's subscribers lived in Syria, the publishers had to be careful not to offend the Turks so much that they would ban the paper's distribution. So after nearly a year as editor, Rihbany left in search of a job where he could express his opinions more freely.

- Rihbany wrote in *A Far Journey* that his experiences with prejudice were "so rare that they are not worth mentioning." However, he did recall that when he married an American woman in about 1895, the *Ohio State Journal* reported the wedding under the headline "An Ohio School Teacher Has Poor Taste."

- Seven years after coming to America, Rihbany visited Syria. "What I had become in the New World could not be easily reconciled to what I had been in the Old World," he wrote in his autobiography. "I felt, as never before, that as an American citizen my religion must be as free, as progressive, and as hopeful as the genius of my adopted country."

For More Information

Rihbany, Abraham Mitrie. *America Save the Near East.* Boston: Beacon Press, 1918.

Rihbany, Abraham Mitrie. *A Far Journey.* Boston: Houghton Mifflin, 1914.

Rihbany, Abraham Mitrie. *Wise Men from the East and from the West.* Boston: Houghton Mifflin, 1922.

Maha Ezzeddine

"What Ramadan Means to Me"

Selection from an essay
Published in 1997 by the American Muslim Council

The month of Ramadan is sacred to Muslims. They believe the prophet Muhammad (c. 570–632), the founder of Islam, received the first of many revelations from God during Ramadan. They set aside this month every year for spiritual growth through self-denial and extra prayer. The self-denial takes the form of fasting; between sunrise and sunset each day, adult Muslims may not eat or drink (not even water). They are also expected to make extra efforts in other forms of self-control, such as not getting angry, avoiding harsh language, and treating other people with respect.

"Fasting is a jihad—struggle—for Muslims," an American Muslim leader, Salam Al-Marayati, wrote in the *Los Angeles Times*. "But I believe that God wants us to realize the potential of human will power." In addition to helping Muslims develop willpower and self-control, fasting makes them more compassionate toward poor people. It also encourages a sense of community, as many Muslims gather with friends or relatives to share the daily evening meal, *iftar,* after sundown. The meal is followed by a nightly prayer that includes reading approximately one-thirtieth of the Koran (so that by the end of

"How thankful we are that we can attend our places of worship so freely in America, without the fear of being arrested, shot or harassed; thankful that we can spend our Ramadan in the one country in which religious freedom is so manifest."

Muslims pray during a Ramadan service in Washington, D.C., January 1997. *Reproduced by permission of AP/Wide World Photos.*

the month each person will have read the entire Muslim holy book). Each morning during Ramadan, Muslims arise early so they can finish a morning meal, *suhoor,* before dawn.

Things to remember while reading "What Ramadan Means to Me":

- *Allah* is the Arabic word for "God." Muslims show respect by adding an expression such as *Subhanahu Wa Ta'ala* each time they say or write Allah. This expression, which may be abbreviated as "swt," means "Allah is pure of having partners and He is exalted from having a son." In other words, Muslims believe there is only one God who has neither partners nor children.

- A *fanous* (lantern) is a traditional symbol of Ramadan. When walking to the mosque (Muslim house of worship) for morning prayer, Muslims used to carry lanterns to light the way in the predawn hours. They also used them when going to the mosque or to a friend's home for evening prayers. Some say that the *fanous* was first used in Egypt more than a thousand years ago to light the way for Muslims who went out to look for the thin crescent of the new moon that marked the first night of Ramadan.

- Fasting during Ramadan is the third of five pillars (basic principles) of Islam. The first pillar is profession of faith by saying "There is no God but Allah, and Muhammad is the prophet [messenger] of Allah"; many Muslims repeat this phrase several times a day. The second pillar is ritual prayer; Muslims must say certain prayers, accompanied by appropriate body movements, five times every day, at dawn, noon, midafternoon, sunset, and night. The fourth pillar is giving money to poor and sick people. The fifth pillar is *hajj* (pilgrimage); all Muslims who are financially and physically able to are expected to travel to Mecca, Muhammad's home, in Saudi Arabia for prayer at least once during their life.

"What Ramadan Means to Me"

The abandoned soccer field is silent and empty except for a small crowd of children scrutinizing the horizon. A few eager men and women stand a small distance away clutching binoculars in their gloved hands. A joyful shout arises from the crowd of shivering children. "I found it! I found it!" exclaims an excited child and a finger points to the sky. Immediately, almost everyone else sees it. Like the glistening of a pearl from a crack in an oyster shell, a thin sliver of moonlight adorns the sky. Squeals of delight escape the children and the men shake hands joyfully. A soft chant comes from the lips of a young boy, "Welcome, welcome, O Ramadan!"

The shimmering "hilal" is the telltale sign of the coming holy month. It is something I look forward to eagerly throughout the year, which in comparison to Ramadan is like a barren desert. For Ramadan is the month in which I am closest to my religion, when I can best experience its joys and rewards. In no other month do I feel so surrounded by Islam and its followers. In no other month does Islamic pride raise its banners so high.

To me, Ramadan is much more than fasting. It is a period of Islamic **rejuvenation,** *in which I set my goals, and then try to go beyond them. It is one of the few times of the year when I am aware of the millions of Muslims besides me, doing what I do, feeling what I feel. Ramadan is a time in which apologies are made, grudges forgotten, new friends embraced, and old friends renewed. Sometime during Ramadan comes that moment when I realize that no place is dearer to me than my* **Masjid.** *During this month, I often reach an ultimate peak, when I feel that my heart has never been closer to Allah (swt).*

Perhaps the most profound difference Ramadan has from the rest of the year, is that instead of attempting to **improvise** *our Islam to fit into America and our lives, we shape America and our lives to fit into Islam. We try to catch our five daily prayers at the Masjid, regardless of our work hours, school schedule or time. Many are driven by an urge to pray the* **Tarawih** *prayers at the Masjid, and are willing to skip valuable homework time and sleep hours to attend them. The constant twinge of hunger reminds us of our duty, and it is not difficult to cut out the distractions of* **Shaytan.** *The television often sits in a dusty corner as the family in another room reads* **Quran.** *In the same way we used to fit prayers in between the hustle of our everyday life, during Ramadan, we fit our life in between our prayers.*

For the child who comes home with a construction paper lantern dangling from his wrist, and for the grandmother who takes her special Quran off the shelf, Ramadan is a "spring cleaning" of character. In Sunday schools, children are taught to control their anger and to give and to be grateful to Allah. Ramadan is a time when many sisters, young and old, decide to adopt the **Hijaab** *as their timeless companion. We discard all bad language from our tongues and try to replace it with a constant flow of* **Dhikr.** *We recognize our mistakes during Ramadan, and work to correct them. He with the* **parsimonious** *greed becomes he of the generous giving, and she of the uncontrollable temper becomes she of the patient understanding. Most importantly, Ramadan is the month in which we beg Allah (swt) for his forgiveness with all our being. For me, Ramadan is a total revising of* **resolutions** *and intentions, which I can only hope that Allah (swt) will purify. . . .*

Living in America only makes Ramadan more cherished. I spend **Iftar** *with the members of the local Masjid; they become my family.*

Rejuvenation: Energizing; refreshment.

Masjid: Mosque (Muslim house of worship).

Improvise: Mold; make fit.

Tarawih: Specific prayers performed during Ramadan.

Shaytan: Satan; devil.

Quran: Also spelled Koran; the Muslim holy book.

Hijaab: (Hijab) clothing that covers a Muslim woman's head and body, except for her face and hands.

Dhikr: Remembrance of Allah.

Parsimonious: Selfish.

Resolutions: Promises; commitments.

Iftar: The breaking of fast.

It is with confidence that we refrain from snacking on chips with our non-Muslim comrades, for we know that we are the pioneers and that our example will set the standard. In no other country does meeting another fasting Muslim in front of a McDonald's offer so much reassurance. . . .

But dearest to me, O Ramadan, are your starlit nights in which we all venture out to our Masjid to worship Allah (swt). The doors of the houses of Allah are open at all times to us, and the recitation of a believer constantly dwells between their walls. In no other country can such eager crowds be found in the Masjids. Muslims across the United States pray in the basements of houses, in old schools, in community centers, and even in greenhouses; places all bestowed with the honor of being a Masjid. In no other country can we attend four **rak'ahs** led by a Jordanian **Imam**, then drive down the highway to complete the other four behind a Pakistani. Late at night, we may decide to go to our local Masjid, where an Egyptian Imam leads the prayer in rotation with

An Iraqi family gathers for a post-sundown meal during Ramadan in Baghdad, Iraq, December 1998. Some Arab American women who do not usually wear the *hijab* will don the traditional scarf during Ramadan. *Reproduced by permission of AP/Wide World Photos.*

Rak'ahs: Units of ritual prayer.

Imam: A Muslim religious leader; a leader of group prayer.

Rak'ah and Salat

Muslims are expected to perform ritual prayer (*salat*) five times each day. They may pray privately or with a group. Before praying, they wash their faces, feet, hands, and arms. They do not wear shoes while praying, and they pray on a prayer rug. Some rugs have a compass attached because Muslims must pray facing east toward Mecca.

Salat consists of sets of actions called *rak'ahs*. According to the organization Answering Islam, each *rak'ah* is performed in this way:

- Standing, the worshiper indicates an intention to pray by touching the ears with the thumbs, holding the palms open, while saying "*Allahu Akbar*" ("God is the greatest"). Lowering the hands to the sides or crossing them on the chest, the worshiper recites a verse from the Koran.

- Bending over and placing the hands on the knees, the worshiper says, "*Allahu Akbar*," and perhaps other expressions, then stands back up.

- The worshiper prostrates himself or herself by placing the toes, knees, palms of hands, and forehead on the ground.

- The worshiper rises to a sitting position with the feet underneath the body and the hands on the thighs. After a few moments, the worshiper prostrates himself or herself a second time and then stands up straight.

Salat normally consists of two *rak'ahs* at dawn, three at sundown, and four at each of the other three designated prayer times. After each *rak'ah* is performed, the worshiper says certain expressions; after completing the assigned number of *rak'ahs,* the worshiper turns the head to one side and says, "*Asalamu Aleikum*" ("peace be upon you").

a Sudanese. How thankful we are that we can attend our places of worship so freely in America, without the fear of being arrested, shot or harassed; thankful that we can spend our Ramadan in the one country in which religious freedom is so **manifest**. The dark skinned prays with his shoulder and feet touching those of the light skinned and the old believer gently lines a learning youth by his side. Nowhere can such varied forms of unity, such acceptance of differences be found as during Ramadan. Few other places have so many people of so many origins humbled themselves with their

Manifest: Apparent.

tears and prayer. This is all a part of our month. The harmony and open-mindedness of Ramadan assures the heart of every Muslim that his religion is from Allah (swt) and that this month is a great blessing. (Ezzeddine, "What Ramadan Means to Me")

What happened next . . .

The end of the Ramadan fast is celebrated with a joyous holiday, *Eid-al-Fitr.* The traditional meal for sundown on the last day of Ramadan begins with dates and includes fried dough balls made with split peas; salads made with chickpeas and onions; and strong, sweet black tea. The following morning, after prayers, there is a banquet that includes chicken, potatoes, fried fish, noodles, lentil soup served over white rice, carrot cake, and other sweets. The holiday lasts three days, during which families gather and children receive money, candy, clothing, and other gifts.

Did you know . . .

- Muslims use a lunar calendar, in which a new month begins with each new moon. There are twelve months, each twenty-nine or thirty days long. There are 354 days per year, rather than the 365 that appear in the popular American calendar. As a result, the month of Ramadan begins eleven days earlier every year.

- Colorful Ramadan lanterns are often made with panes of stained glass, and they are usually decorated with inscriptions, such as verses from the Koran. Modern ones may also contain battery-powered devices that play recorded messages like *Allahu Ahkbar* (God is the greatest).

- Ezzeddine's paper "What Ramadan Means to Me" won the annual essay contest of the American Muslim Council in 1997.

For More Information

Al-Marayati, Salam. "Ramadan: Fasting for Spiritual Reflection, Renewal." *Los Angeles Times,* January 11, 1997. Available on the Muslim Public Affairs Council Web site at http://www.mpac.org/opinion/art007.html (May 1999).

Ezzeddine, Maha. "What Ramadan Means to Me." Available on the American Muslim Council Web site at http://www.amermuslim.org/publish/op/op-ezzedine.html (February 1999).

"Salat." *Answering Islam* Available at http://www.answering-islam.org/Index/S/salat.html (June 1999).

Nezar Andary

"American Druze Youth Issues & Concerns"
***Our Heritage* article**
Published in 1990

Children and grandchildren of immigrants face the challenge of combining their ethnic heritage and their American birth into a personal identity. This is especially difficult for Druze youth because their culture centers on a religion that has remained largely secret for centuries—even from most of its members.

The Druze faith is described by Abdallah Najjar, a prominent American Druze, as being "a protestant movement in Islam." Najjar told Muslim scholar Yvonne Haddad, as quoted in *The Muslim World,* "We Druze are Islamic but not Muslim." Since it split from mainstream Islam about 1020 A.D., Druzism has kept details of its beliefs secret for two main reasons. First, it was a way of protecting its followers from religious persecution; some Druze now believe that secrecy is no longer necessary in countries where they are not being persecuted. Second, the religion is a mystical one that cannot be understood logically; only those who have proved their commitment and readiness to know more are given access to its deeper messages. A third consideration is that, unlike Mus-

> "Other religions have more outlets for information. That, however, should not hinder us in searching for truth."

The Biblical patriarch Abraham walking with his son, Isaac. The major holiday observed by the Druze is *Eid al-Adha* (Feast of Sacrifice), which celebrates the willingness of Abraham to obey God's command to sacrifice his son. *Reproduced by permission of Archive Photos.*

lims, the Druze believe in separation of church and state, and they consider religion a personal, private matter.

American Druze began to organize in 1907, and they have held national conventions since 1914. In 1947 they formed a truly national organization that is now known as the American Druze Society (ADS). By 1970 the society realized it needed to refocus its activities and goals in order to attract more young, American-born members. The ADS undertook several new projects, including establishing a Committee on Religious Affairs (CORA), which began to publish books explaining Druze history and faith. About 1980 the ADS began publishing *Our Heritage,* a quarterly magazine that explores Druze history, religion, and culture.

In 1989 the ADS began developing a youth program that would include educational, social, and athletic activities. Nezar Andary, a leader of the American Druze Youth organization, volunteered to help. At the 1990 ADS national convention, Andary introduced radio personality Casey Kasem, who spoke to the youth group about growing up Arab American. In an article published in *Our Heritage* in 1990, Andary explained his concerns and ideas about searching for his identity as a Druze American.

Things to remember while reading "American Druze Youth Issues & Concerns":

- The major holiday observed by the Druze is *Eid al-Adha* (Feast of Sacrifice). This holiday, which is also the most important feast for Muslims, celebrates the willingness of Abraham (a major figure in the Jewish, Christian, and Muslim religions) to obey God's command to sacrifice his son. As Abraham was about to kill his son, God told him to stop and to sacrifice an animal instead. The traditional Druze celebration includes fireworks, a festive banquet, and donations of food to the poor.

- People become members of the Druze community by birth. They believe that when a Druze dies, he or she is immediately reincarnated (reborn) as another Druze of the same gender (sex). Their faith is not open to receiving converts, so historically they had no reason or desire to explain their beliefs to outsiders. However, in the United States, the free exchange of information is important and commonplace, and American Druze realize that explaining their faith in general terms improves their public image. This became particularly important during the Lebanese civil war of the 1980s, when Americans tended to support the Christian side, which they understood, rather than the Druze side, which they did not.

"American Druze Youth Issues & Concerns"

American Druze Society

When I was first asked to represent the Arab-American Druze Youth on this panel, my first reaction was Hey! How can I do this?

Yes, I am Arab-American and yes I am Druze and yes I am an eigh-teen-year-old youth. . . But how can I represent the Young Druze of America? All I could think of was the vast differences of all the Druze Youth. We may be country dwellers or from the city, we may be Northerners or Southerners, Californians or Texans. Some of us have been in America for three generations, some parents just came here twenty years ago and there are many others, and that seems to me is the dilemma that confronts us all.

*We need common **denominators** in order to create a strong unity between us. We have them though. We are all Americans. We are all Arabs and we are all Druze. Should this be enough to make us feel at ease with ourselves? Unfortunately, there are many serious questions and issues that many of us feel are standing in our way.*

*One of my goals is to **enumerate** just a few challenges that I have constantly heard from many parents, friends and relatives.*

Identity

We have four identities that we must learn how to relate to. Sometimes we want to be more American, sometimes we want to be more Arab, sometimes more Druze, sometimes more Lebanese, Palestinian, Syrian, or Jordanian. At times for me, I do not want to identify with any of them. I just want to be a citizen of the world if that's possible. Our many identities should not be a difficult problem because they all have features with which we can be proud.

The reality of all this is that the addition of our American society creates a critical imbalance for young Druze Americans. The prob-lem is how do we adapt our rich Middle Eastern heritage and reli-gion to American lifestyles . . . as Americans, as Arabs and as Druze.

The Community

In the Middle East, the Druze are extremely close knit. They all live in the same areas and villages. There is a distinct Druze commu-nity. I do not believe those kind of communities exist in the U.S. We all are spread apart. In some places, however, there are large groups of families who are close, but this is still not the same. For many of us, we find ourselves being a minority of one [in] some areas. The closest Druze family to our family in New Hampshire is about 200 miles away. I am sure that there are many other families like ours. Even if there are nine or ten families that live in one area, the lifestyle and others in the communities change the way we live dras-tically from the rural community of Lebanon, Syria, or Palestine.

Denominators: Traits.

Enumerate: Delineate; outline.

What we obviously need is more communication. We are not living the same lifestyles that the Druze previously lived for centuries. Therefore, one convention a year is not enough to fully **comprehend** our heritage.

Faith

The most significant question arises with young Druze while discussing what exactly is our religion about? Most of us young adults who have been exposed to Druze teaching and history often receive mixed messages. If we talk to some of our elder relatives, we may hear that our religion is secret and we therefore can't know it while living here [in America]. Others say we must learn Arabic to truly understand our religion. Our parents try to teach us the religion, but to our dismay we learn from our friends that their parents taught something vastly different. As we become older, we begin to encounter many discussions concerning religion. We need to understand and know that Faith **transcends** languages and the universal soul knows no language! Many of us find ourselves floundering to explain the depth and logic of our basic beliefs. Quite simply other religions have more outlets for information. That, however, should not hinder us in searching for truth. We still have options and should not use lack of information as an excuse for doing nothing.

- *We can try the libraries.*
- *CORA has written four books. Is that enough?*
- *Treasured **Hikma**, why not a translation? Maybe one day the Hikma can be translated, but for now we will have to do the best with what we have.*

This lack of information, though, makes most people not even want to think about religion.

"No place of worship or meeting." For years I have heard many complaints that the Druze have no place to pray like other religions. Of course, in the Middle East there is the **Majlis**, but here we have nothing. We should have many Druze centers throughout America.

Another fact that I see is that we never find young devout Druze. In Lebanon, we do. We do not have any role models. There is not one Arab-American Druze **Sheikh** who is willing to work full time helping others with the religion. Or again, does this mean we have to go back to the Middle East?

There are missing links. Why do I see many Druze families celebrating Christmas? Do we really celebrate our only holiday in the

Comprehend: Fully understand.

Transcends: Rises above.

Hikma: The collection of sacred Druze texts is called *al-Hikma al-Sharifa* (Epistles of Wisdom).

Majlis: A Druze place of worship.

Sheikh: Religious leader.

correct manner? Many questions seem infinite. Let us look at ourselves in a different way, but more positive. We need to strengthen our faith, traditions, and rituals in America because they are what can keep us together. In the Middle East, people have used a unique and rich culture to overshadow the religion. This culture keeps them together. Unfortunately, American society moves us farther away from that culture. Thus, we must strengthen our religious beliefs in order to have a better understanding of who we are. We need to find a way to make our Druze religion workable and compatible with American society. I am not suggesting that we begin a new religion or change our basic Druze religion. We need to know the true Druze religion. I just want to be able to say, "I am an Arab-American Druze" and know what that means. As young Druze, we can no longer just ask our parents and others for help. We have to take the thousand year flame of the Druze history and make it burn in America forever.

Finally, I hope I have related some issues that are of concern to the American Druze. As individuals, I know that we are one of the most talented minorities in this country. Our parents have given us values and pride in order to survive in this crazy world. Today, I have discussed many of the challenges of being an Arab-American Druze. Never, however, should we hide our heritage for we have much of which we can be proud. (Andary, Our Heritage, *pp. 34-35)*

What happened next . . .

In 1991 Andary helped reorganize the ADS youth group. The following year he served on the organizing committee for the ADS national convention; one of the featured speakers was a prominent Druze sheikh from Lebanon who spoke about the Druze faith and held discussions with young people.

The first step in establishing the Druze centers Andary envisioned was accomplished in 1993, when the ADS celebrated the grand opening of its first cultural center, located in the southern California city of Eagle Rock. The center includes a Druze library, a recreation room, a Majlis, and space for events like family celebrations or public lectures. The American

Differences between Druze and Muslim Beliefs

The Druze faith is based on the doctrines of Islam, but it interprets those doctrines in a less literal, more symbolic way. The seven pillars (basic principles) of the Druze faith are:

1. Profession of faith, which is done not only by words but also by actions .

2. Prayer, which is a personal activity of drawing nearer to God rather than a precisely defined ritual

3. Charity, which includes various ways of helping the Druze community and its members—for example, giving money or food, providing advice, or showing a good example of attitude and lifestyle

4. Fasting, which means abstaining from anything that distracts one from unity with God

5. Pilgrimage, which is a journey to the House of Knowledge of the unity with God, rather than a literal journey to a physical place

6. *Jihad*, which is personal striving for a state of peace and contentment, not a physical "holy war" (which is what most Americans think *jihad* means)

7. Allegiance (obedience or commitment) to the authority of the Druze leaders, which leads to seeing God's presence in all things

---

Druze Foundation (ADF), a fund-raising organization formed in 1989 to sponsor cultural and religious projects, plans to establish similar centers in other parts of the country.

In 1994 CORA published Andary's book *On Druze Identity.* Between 1996 and 1998 Andary, who was a graduate student in literature at the University of California at Los Angeles (UCLA), contributed ten articles to *Al Jadid,* an Arab American magazine; they included translations of Arabic poetry and part of an Arabic play. In one of his articles, Andary wrote about the importance of reading translations of Arabic articles, poetry, and fiction in order to really understand Arab culture. In 1999 Andary spoke at the first national convention of the Institute of Druze Studies (IDS); his topic was "Al-Hakim in Modern Literature." Al-Hakim bi-Amr Allah (996–1021) was the founder of Druzism.

During the 1990s the ADS and some newer American Druze organizations opened Internet Web sites to make information more widely available. They include *ADS* (http://www.druze.com), the *Institute of Druze Studies* (http://www.idspublications.com), and the *Young Druze Professionals* (http://www.ydp.com).

Did you know . . .

- The word *Druze* came from an early leader named Muhammad ibn-Ismail al-Darazi. Because al-Darazi tried to make himself more powerful by changing the religion's teachings, he is now considered a traitor to the faith. Another name that is sometimes used instead of Druze is *Muwahhidoon,* which means *monotheistic* (people who believe there is only one God).

- The Druze faith is also known as *Tawhid* (unity). The movement began with al-Hakim's desire to formulate a set of religious doctrines that Christians, Jews, and Muslims could all agree on.

- Most Druze are *juhhal* (ignorant or uninitiated); they know a limited amount about their faith. Members who show notable devotion and spirituality may undertake special training; those who successfully complete this lengthy process become members of the *uqqal* (wise, initiated). About one-fifth of Druze members become *uqqal;* roughly 30 percent of the *uqqal* are women. Through continuing study, the *uqqal* eventually learn the full doctrine of the faith, and they participate in secret prayer services on behalf of the *juhhal.*

For More Information

Andary, Nezar. "American Druze Youth Issues & Concerns." *Our Heritage,* Fall 1990.

Andary, Nezar. *On Druze Identity.* New York: American Druze Society, 1994.

Haddad, Yvonne. "The Druze in North America." *The Muslim World,* April 1991, pp. 111–32.

Najjar, Dr. Abdallah. "The Muwahhidoon Druze—Synopsis of an Islamic Sect." *Young Druze Professionals Newsletter,* December 1, 1997. Available at http://www.ydp.com/ydpn1003.htm (October 20, 1999).

Index

Arafat, Yasir 47, 56, 60, 151,
154–55
Arens, Mosheh 54–55
Asfahani, Magdoline 91, **119–26**
Aswad, Barbara C. 148, 151–52,
155–56

B

Balfour Declaration 46
"Banned Poem" 59–65
Barak, Ehud 151, 155
**"Blaming Bombing on Muslims
Shows Prevalence of Preju-
dice" 111–18**
"The Body, in Several Languages"
197
Boston, Massachusetts 21–22,
25–31
**"Boundaries: Arab/American"
191–98**
Bozieh, Ibtisam 62
Bread and Roses Strike (1912) 23
Brooklyn, New York 33–38

C

Censorship 60–63, 76
Chaldeans 30, 209
Christians 30, 36, 56–57, 68,
113–14, 119, 122, 141, 145,
148, 152, 172, 183, 187,
198–201, 203, 205–09, 223,
228
Christmas 205–06
Civil rights 89–146
Cold War 105, 139
Committee on Religious Affairs
(CORA) 222, 225, 228
Communism 48, 139
Coptic Orthodox Church 209
Council on American-Islamic Re-
lations (CAIR) 116–18
*Crusading Doctor: My Fight for
Cooperative Medicine*
103–09

D

Daoud, Mojahid 68, 81–88
*Day of the Long Night: A Pales-
tinian Refugee Remembers
the Nakba* 45–50
"Dead Are My People" 5–10
Dearborn, Michigan 72, 172
Discrimination 89–146, 147–48
Druzism 200–01, 221–28
**"Dying with the Wrong Name"
157–66**

E

Eid al-Adha 223
Eid-al-Fitr 219
Eisenlohr, Charlene 171–79
Ellis Island, New York 158–59,
162 (ill.), 163
English language proficiency 22,
28
Entrepreneurship 35–38
Epiphany 206–07
Executive Decision 119
Ezzeddine, Maha 201, **213–20**

F

Factory workers 21–23
Fall River, Massachusetts 20–21
Fanous 214–15, 219
A Far Journey **203–11**
Farrakhan, Louis 200
Fasting 213–19, 227
Federal Bureau of Investigation
(FBI) 83, 93, 96, 131, 134,
141, 144
**"First Generation Americans:
The Bridge between Yester-
day and Tomorrow" 25–31**
Five pillars of Islam 215
**Foreign Intelligence Surveil-
lance Act (FISA)** 91, **93–102**

G

Garment industry 20–23

N

O

P

Q

R

S